# Teens'
## Guide
### for a
## Purposeful
## Life

Jenny Anticoli

Ellen P. Blooming

Steve Sherwood

Publications International, Ltd.

**Jenny Anticoli** is a trained youth minister and served as Director for Youth Ministry at First Presbyterian Church in Prosser, Washington. Currently, she is a freelance writer and regularly contributes to Passageway.org, the teen division of the Billy Graham Evangelistic Association.

**Ellen P. Blooming, Ph.D.,** has contributed to many inspirational books for children, teens, and adults, including *God's Promises to Teens, My Little Prayer Book,* and *Blessed by an Angel.* She is also a contributing editor for *Discovery Girl Magazine,* where she writes an advice column, in addition to other feature articles.

**Steve Sherwood** has been involved in youth ministry for almost 20 years and is currently the regional director of Young Life, where he meets with children and teens and trains young staff members in youth ministry.

**Consultant: Gary Burge** is a professor in the department of Biblical and Theological Studies at Wheaton College. He holds a Ph.D. in New Testament from King's College, The University of Aberdeen in Aberdeen, Scotland, and a master of divinity degree from Fuller Theological Seminary. He is a member of the Biblical Archaeological Society, the Society of Biblical Literature, and the Institute for Biblical Research.

**Youth Ministry Consultant: Amy Britton** has been involved in Youth Ministry for several years, leading Bible studies and training other young adults in Youth Ministry. She is currently the Junior High Youth Director at the Glen Ellyn Evangelical Covenant Church and is studying Christian Formation and Ministry at Wheaton College.

Illustrations by Margaret Freed and Marty Harris.


ACKNOWLEDGMENTS:

Unless otherwise noted, all scripture quotations are taken from the *New Revised Standard Version* of the Bible. Copyright © 1989 by the Division of Christian Education of the National Council of the Churches of Christ in the United States of America. Used by permission. All rights reserved.

Scripture quotations marked LB are taken from *The Living Bible.* Copyright © 1971. Used by permission of Tyndale House Publishers, Inc. All rights reserved.

Scripture quotations marked NIV are taken from *The Holy Bible, New International Version.* Copyright © 1973, 1978, 1984, International Bible Society. Used by permission of Zondervan Publishing House. All rights reserved.

Scripture quotations marked NLT are taken from *The Holy Bible, New Living Translation.* Copyright © 1996. Used by permission of Tyndale House Publishers, Inc., Wheaton, Illinois 60187. All rights reserved.

Louis Weber, CEO
Publications International, Ltd.
7373 North Cicero Avenue
Lincolnwood, Illinois 60712

Permission is never granted for commercial purposes.

Manufactured in China.

8 7 6 5 4 3 2 1

ISBN: 1-4127-1059-6

Library of Congress Control Number: 2004110633

# Contents

# FINDING PURPOSE

All of us want to figure out how to make life work. How to get on the team, how to find good friends, how to program the VCR. One of the most exciting and terrifying things about being a teen is that for the first time you are beginning to find your own answers to life's questions. Who am I? Is there a reason I'm here? Where am I going? Is there a God? If so, what is he like and what does he think of me?

That's what this book is all about. If you are looking for an answer to what major to choose in college, you won't find it here. If you are looking for answers that don't require any thought, work, or commitment, this isn't the book for you.

If you want bigger answers, or at least help in getting pointed in the right direction, this book can help. If you've ever sat around and ached to do something that really made a difference, you'll find some help in these essays.

This book is about purpose. It's about discovering that God made you on purpose, discovering that God has purposes for the entire world, and discovering how to begin living a life filled with meaning and purpose.

Here's how it works. There are 52 topics in this book, which, by an amazing coincidence, match the number of weeks in the year. We'd like to encourage you to take

one section and "live in it" for a whole week. The topics are short enough that you could read one while eating a bowl of cereal. At the same time, they have enough meat that they can give you things to think about for several days. So, take your time. Read each topic several times in a week before moving on.

Each topic has at least one if not several quotes from the Bible. Don't skim over these to get to the essays. The essays are our best thoughts about life's questions, but the Bible is God's message to humanity. It has encouraged, comforted, and challenged people for thousands of years. The hope is that not only will you read the verses quoted in the book, but you'll also want to find out more about what the Bible has to say about life, the world we live in, and God.

You'll also notice that each topic ends with a prayer, which doesn't have lots of fancy words. No "thou" or "thus speaketh." The prayers are in plain language, so you talk to God just like you'd talk to a friend. Use these prayers as starting points, but don't feel you have to stop there. God loves to have us talk to him any time we want and however we feel comfortable.

Finally, you probably don't eat the same food every day. Same with this book. Jump around. What you need this week is going to be different from what is going on six months from now.

We've included stuff here to make you laugh and make you think. Mostly we've included stuff that will point you to the God who gives life purpose and has great plans for you!

# THE WORLD WE LIVE IN

There are so many mysteries in this wild, wonderful life. How do we find a sense of purpose and happiness? How do we make sense of the events and relationships around us? How do we figure out right from wrong? Confusing stuff sometimes.

If you want to understand your car, go to the maker who built it. Which is true with life, too. God is the great and wise creator who put our amazing world together. As soon as you read these essays, experience the wonder of God in your relationships and in the world around you.

# God Delights in Us

> **Try to realize what this means—
> the Lord is God! He made us—
> we are his people, the sheep
> of his pasture.**
> **PSALM 100:3 LB**

Janelle was depressed. Life just wasn't going according to plan. She didn't get into the college she wanted. Her grades weren't as good as they had been in junior high. She couldn't seem to find a boyfriend, and her parents wouldn't even get her a car! She had stopped going to church, and the thought of saying a prayer was the furthest thing from her mind. If you'd tried to tell her that she was God's creation and he took delight in her, she would've laughed in your face!

---

## WE ARE HIS CHILDREN

GOD, OUR FATHER, NEVER TURNS HIS BACK ON HIS CHILDREN, NO MATTER WHAT WE SAY, NO MATTER WHAT WE DO. WE ARE HIS DIVINE CREATION, AND WE CANNOT ESCAPE FROM HIS LIGHT. (WHY WOULD YOU WANT TO?) HE LOVES US AND DELIGHTS IN US AND ENCOURAGES US. GOD BELIEVES THAT WE WILL ULTIMATELY LISTEN TO HIM TO FIND THE WAY THAT IS TRUE AND RIGHT.

---

**BIBLE BITS & BYTES**

For the Lord will not forsake his people; he will not abandon his heritage.

PSALM 94:14

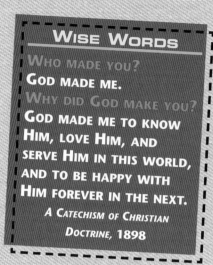

Do you ever feel like that? What's wrong with her point of view? Well, you guessed it. First off, it's not *her* plan for her life, it's his! The Lord has an amazing plan for all of us, but it may not involve the per-fect boyfriend or a fancy car. We have to focus on all the good in our life—all the gifts he places in our everyday lives. And then, ask what we can do for him to fulfill his plan!

The totally amazing thing is that even when we feel like Janelle did, God *still* delights in us! Pretty cool, huh? Come on, think

about it. Think about some time when you got in trouble with your parents. (There have been a ton of times, right?) They were upset. They were angry. They might have been disappointed. But you are their child. They still loved you and took delight in you as their own. Really. Parents love their child, and God is our Father in heaven. He wants us to succeed and be happy and take good care of each other and his earth. He wants to take delight in his creation.

**10 REASONS GOD DELIGHTS IN ME!**

1.
2.
3.
4.
5.
6.
7.
8.
9.
10.

I WAS CREATED TO BRING JOY TO MY FATHER.
AND JOY I WILL BRING.
LET HIS NAME BE PRAISED BY ALL LIVING THINGS!
IN THE DARKNESS OF NIGHT,
I REMEMBER THAT HE CREATED ME TO EXPERIENCE THE LIGHT.

**Hey God!**
If you're so delighted in me, how come you make life so hard? Some days I just feel like you've got it in for me. I mean, so many things seem to be going wrong. Maybe I shouldn't feel like this, but sometimes I do. I pray that you will help me get through these feelings and find a way back to your goodness and light. I do believe that everything will get better. And yes, I know that all the stuff that bugs me isn't really all *that* difficult compared to what other people have to live with every day. So please help me, God. Help me remember that you are my Father, and remind me that it is my job to serve you with my life as best I can.
**Amen**

So, okay. What does all this have to do with *anything?* The whole point is that God created us and he takes delight in us—so shouldn't *we* be taking delight in ourselves and in each other? You bet! So the question is: How do you continue on that path if you're already doing it, or how do you get started if all this is new to you?

**BIBLE BITS & BYTES**
God told Noah to build the ark 300 cubits long and 50 cubits wide. So what's a cubit? A cubit is the measurement from the tip of the middle finger of a grown man to his elbow—about 17½ inches long. A royal cubit was longer, about 20½ inches.

## GOD TAKES DELIGHT IN MY LIGHT!

### A WALK WITH THE LORD

GO SOMEWHERE QUIET AND BEAUTIFUL—A PARK, A LAKE, EVEN YOUR BACK-YARD. SPEND AT LEAST TEN MINUTES WALKING WITH GOD. NO FRIENDS, NO PETS, JUST YOU—AND HIM. OPEN YOUR MIND. OPEN YOUR HEART. DON'T ASK FOR ANYTHING! JUST LISTEN. LISTEN TO WHAT HE WANTS TO SHARE WITH YOU. LISTEN TO WHAT HE WANTS YOU TO DO.

First off, of course, comes faith and belief that we truly are his children. Pray to God as "Father," and try thinking of him as a compassionate parent who always loves, accepts, and trusts us—no matter what. Remember, remember, remember, and beside that, never for-get—our Father only gives us what we can handle. So even if life seems to be looking kinda grim for awhile, you know you're gonna get

THE HOLY SPIRIT KNOWS THAT INSIDE US—WITHIN OUR SPIRIT, OUR SOUL—WE ARE FIRST AND FOREMOST GOD'S CHILDREN. THIS REMINDS US TO PUT GOD FIRST AND LIVE OUR LIVES TO MAKE OUR FATHER PROUD!

**SHAMPOO DELIGHT**

Use Shampoo Delight when you feel that God has turned his back or when things aren't going well.

INSTRUCTIONS: Apply shampoo liberally. Wash hair, and rinse until all negative feelings are washed away. This may take several minutes to several hours.

CAUTION: Lots of negative feelings may cause drain blockage! When finished, your outlook will be positive. You will appreciate God's love for you.

through it and be even stronger and brighter and filled with more faith.

Next, all that's required is a slight attitude adjustment. If God is going to take delight in your life, you have to live in a positive, uplifting way—every day! And the way to start doing that is to begin with great thoughts and put them into action. Say this every morning when you wake up: "I'm going to live today so that God will truly take delight in me!" Then pass out the sunglasses because you're absolutely going to shine!

## KEEP YOUR POSITIVE ATTITUDE GLOWING

A flashlight won't just keep on going forever and ever (in spite of what those commercials might lead us to believe!). Nope. You've gotta change the batteries once in awhile—and maybe even get a new lightbulb. The same goes for your positive light that shines for

God. Every so often evaluate your attitude—listen
to the words that come
out of your mouth. Do
you say and think posi-
tive, upbeat comments?
If you find yourself
slipping, just pause
for a moment and
change your mental batteries.
Things will be looking brighter in no time!

## BIBLE BITS & BYTES

For his Holy Spirit speaks to us deep in our hearts and tells us that we are God's children.

ROMANS 8:16 NLT

## PRAYING FOR PURPOSE

> " For the Father himself loves you, because you have loved me and have believed that I came from God. "
> JOHN 16:27

**Dear Father,**
Thank you for creating me as one of
your children and for being such a terrific Father! Help me live up to all your
expectations and bring you nothing but
joy and delight as I live my life. Allow
me to serve you and to do your will so
that I may help bring your word to others. I want them to see how much you
love your children. I will try my best to live to make
you proud of me.
**Amen**

# Even Though We Sin, We Are Loved

" The Lord is merciful and gracious, slow to anger and abounding in steadfast love. He will not always accuse, nor will he keep his anger forever. He does not deal with us according to our sins, nor repay us according to our iniquities. "

**PSALM 103:8-10**

**Dear Father,**

I pray for your forgiveness for what I did today. I know it was wrong, and I feel so bad about it. Help me focus on learning from my mistake and asking for forgiveness, rather than wishing I could go back in time and undo it.

Father, I promise to put you first from now on. To live each day so you'll be proud and not *have* to forgive me. I've learned from today, and I thank you so much for your compassion and understanding.

Give me the courage to tell my parents, even though I know they won't be happy. But I know that they, too, love me, and everything they do is because they want me to learn and grow up to lead a life based on your teachings.

I'm so very sorry, Father. Please accept my request for your forgiveness for my sins.

**Amen**

Let's listen to James's story.

*I'm James, and I had a drink last night. I'm underage, and I've sworn to my parents that I would never drink. And worse than that, I got into my car and drove myself home. When I got home, I lied to my parents about where I'd been and what I'd done. Now I feel really horrible. I'm just so bummed out. I don't know what to do or whom to turn to. How can I turn to God knowing that what I've done is wrong on so many levels? Knowing that I've sinned?*

*I didn't mean for it to happen. I was just hanging out with my best friend, Gary. He came over, and we were playing some computer games. Then he asked if I'd drive him home. Then he asked me to come in. I didn't even realize that his parents were out with his little sister. The house was empty. Of course, we've been home alone before. Our parents trust us. Guess they shouldn't.*

*We were joking around about a big fight that Gary had with his girlfriend earlier in the day, and he said, "I need a drink." We laughed. Then he looked at me and told me to follow him into the family room. His Dad has a bar there. He said we should try it. I thought he was joking. He wasn't. He poured us both drinks. I said, "No thanks," but he just laughed at me. "Come on, we can handle it." I didn't really want to do it, but I didn't say no. I just picked up the glass and drank it. It didn't even taste good. It burned my throat. I wish I could turn back time and walk out of Gary's house before I ever took that drink...*

The thing is, we can't turn back time. You know that, of course. But if you're tempted to do something you know is wrong— that you know you'll regret—you need to think about it again. Try to imagine what the next day will be like. And the day after that. You can *never* go back. Still, we all make bad decisions. We all sin. It comes from having that free will that God gave us. We can't expect ourselves to be perfect, so we have to believe in God and have faith in his forgiveness.

**BIBLE BITS & BYTES**
Many Hebrew and Aramaic words are used by us today when we worship. Hosanna was shouted at Jesus as he come into Jerusalem; it originally meant "Save us!" Amen is Hebrew for "Surely! So be it!" Maranatha is an Aramaic word used by Paul, and it means "Our Lord, come!"

I DID SOMETHING STUPID TODAY. BUT IT'S GONNA BE OKAY. BECAUSE I'M SMART ENOUGH TO KNOW THAT I SHOULDN'T HAVE DONE IT. AND BECAUSE I'M SMART ENOUGH TO KNOW THAT I NEED TO ASK THE LORD FOR GUIDANCE AND FORGIVENESS. AND BECAUSE I KNOW THAT EVERYBODY DOES STUPID THINGS SOMETIMES.

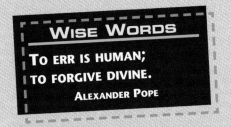
The key is to believe in ourselves. You have to know that you were doing the best you could do at that moment—and that comes from living every day according to his plan. Next, you have to forgive yourself. Then, the really big thing is talking to God about what you did. He wants us to come to him to confess our sins, and he wants to forgive us. God is a loving and nurturing Father, and he knows we will learn and grow as we go through life. Sometimes the lessons we learn from our mistakes might be really difficult or painful. But we've got to swallow our pride, admit we were wrong, and learn something. And we've got to believe that we are forgiven.

He doesn't want us to live in the past. He delights in our experience of the

## FORGIVENESS

Take immediately after sin has occurred. Take only as directed and as seldom as possible. After consuming, notify our Father in heaven through prayer, followed by con-sultation with parents. Any additional antidote will be administered at that time.

**Most effective if taken alone.**

Warning: Keep out of reach of innocent children.

17

## GOD DOESN'T HOLD A GRUDGE.

present. We are obligated to live every day in praise of him and in delight of ourselves. When you've sinned, talk to God. And then be sure to *listen*. Listen with your heart, with your soul, with every part of yourself. It might take time to hear what he has to say. But he will guide you. You will hear it. Listen as he reminds you of his love and forgiveness. Listen as he helps you learn from your sins.

What did James hear when he listened in prayer to his Father in heaven? He learned that he

needed to talk with his parents—to confess to them—and take his punishment. He felt reassured by the Lord that he is loved—by both his parents here on earth and his Father in heaven. And he knew that he had learned something important. The next time he *will* walk away.

God believes in James. God believes in you.

## FORGIVE YOUR SINS?

Sometimes, you might just feel that God has no reason to forgive you. The thing to do at those times is to stop and take stock. Try filling out the list below with five more reasons why God will forgive you when you sin. We've gotten you started!

1. *He created me in his image.*
2. *He takes delight in my life.*
3.
4.
5.
6.
7.

## PRAYING FOR PURPOSE

> **Come now, let us argue it out, says the Lord: though your sins are like scarlet, they shall be like snow; though they are red like crimson, they shall become like wool.**
> **ISAIAH 1:18**

**Lord,**

I walk in your light. And I am honored to be one of your children. Today, I tried to be a child you could be proud of. I did a pretty good job. Not perfect. But not too bad, either! I pray that you will guide me through the night and into tomorrow, that I may keep focused on the path you have set out for me. I know that, with your guidance, I can follow the path of good. Thank you, Lord.
**Good night.**

# Uniquely, Wonderfully Human

" So God created humankind in his image, in the image of God he created them; male and female he created them. "
**GENESIS 1:27**

My dog, Gus, is a totally happy guy. He lives in a loving home. He eats regularly. He sleeps pretty much whenever he wants. He goes out anytime he asks (except during the middle of the night). Sometimes I wish I could just be Gus for a day or three. It would be so easy. No

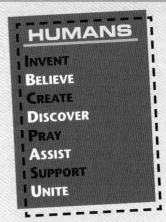

**HUMANS**

I INVENT
I BELIEVE
I CREATE
I DISCOVER
I PRAY
I ASSIST
I SUPPORT
I UNITE

hassles. No pressures. No homework!

Yeah, it sure sounds appealing at times to give up all the daily annoyances of being human. But really, I guess we're pretty lucky. We humans were created in God's image. He didn't create any other creatures to be like him—only us. In doing so, he gave us some pretty interesting abilities and options. I mean, we can choose to go get any kind of fast food we want for lunch! We can study for tests or just let luck be our guide. We can smile at people during the day or be a total grump. Choices. Yes. I think that's the biggest difference between us and all the other animals. We can make choices about anything and everything—what to wear, what to do, what to think...

Every day we distinguish ourselves from the other animals on earth in so very many ways. Of course, probably the most important things we can do that other animals cannot are pray and have faith. Prayer is what gives the strength and the direction to make good use of the free will that separates us from other creatures. Faith is what keeps us going even when the situations and choices seem really

**BIBLE BITS & BYTES**

So be careful to do what the Lord your God has commanded you; do not turn aside to the right or to the left. Walk in all the way that the Lord your God has commanded you, so that you may live and prosper and prolong your days in the land that you will possess.

DEUTERONOMY 5:32–33 NIV

difficult. There are so many choices we *can* make but shouldn't. It's part of what keeps life exciting and challenging—what makes us human. We can do good or evil, help or hurt ourselves, take control of our lives or

just be blown about and not make use of the choices we are given.

When you think about it, a lot of negative choices humans have made distinguish us from other creatures in ways that we can't be very

**Dear Lord,**

Thank you for making me unique among all your magnificent creatures. Help make me worthy of such a life by following your words and sharing the message of your amazing love. Thank you for allowing me to make my own decisions and for trusting me to make good ones. I pray to be worthy of the responsibility of taking care of this beautiful earth and looking out for all your other creatures. When I come to a difficult decision, help me find your guidance and make the correct choice.
**Amen**

**H**APPY TO HELP EACH OTHER

**U**NDERSTANDING OF
ANOTHER'S PROBLEMS

**M**AKING CHOICES

**A**BLE TO PRAY AND ASK FOR
GUIDANCE

**N**EVER GIVE UP THE RIGHTS
AND RESPONSIBILITIES OF
BEING HUMAN!

proud of. Humans are the only animals who wage war against each other. We're also the only ones who destroy our own environment unnecessarily. We judge each other and sometimes force others do what *we* want them to do. Just look at our history books—humans have often been bad animals making bad choices.

**BIBLE BITS & BYTES**

Let us therefore no longer pass judgment on one another, but resolve instead never to put a stumbling block or hindrance in the way of another.

ROMANS 14:13

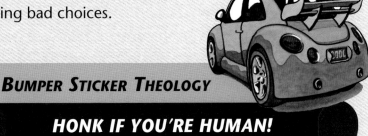

*BUMPER STICKER THEOLOGY*

*HONK IF YOU'RE HUMAN!*

But how to know what to do? Ask God, of course! He created us in his image to be like him—to do good, to make a difference on this earth—to be good animals making the choices he expects. Try saying a prayer each morning, asking for guidance for the day. Ask to appreciate the life he's given you and use it well. And let him know that you are open to doing his good will here on earth. We have the option of helping or hurting and destroying our planet and each other. Let's choose to make a positive difference! What if every person on the earth was dedicated to choosing a path that would make God proud? We could move mountains!

## APPRECIATE THE FACT THAT YOU CAN CHOOSE YOUR OWN PATH!

### SCAVENGER HUNT

THE TASK: SEARCH FOR THE QUALITIES AND ACTIONS THAT MAKE HUMANS UNIQUE

TOOLS NEEDED: NEWS-PAPER, 2 HIGHLIGHTERS (DIFFERENT COLORS)

READ THROUGH THE NEWSPAPER. USE ONE COLOR TO HIGHLIGHT THE WAYS HUMANS ARE DISTIN-GUISHING THEMSELVES FROM OTHER ANIMALS BY MAKING GOOD CHOICES. USE ANOTHER COLOR TO HIGH-LIGHT THE NEGATIVE THINGS HUMANS ARE DOING.

# TEN WAYS TO BE A GOOD HUMAN

1. Smile
2. Appreciate today
3. Inspire someone
4. Pick up some litter
5. Help a friend make a good choice
6. Be respectful
7. Admit you made a bad choice
8. Take special care of a pet
9. Compliment someone
10. Say a prayer

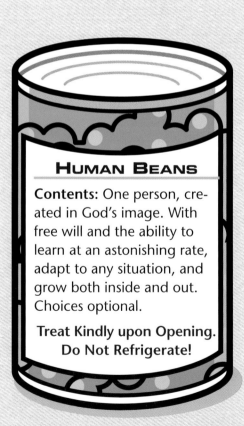

## HUMAN BEANS

**Contents:** One person, created in God's image. With free will and the ability to learn at an astonishing rate, adapt to any situation, and grow both inside and out. Choices optional.

**Treat Kindly upon Opening. Do Not Refrigerate!**

### WISE WORDS

THE TRUE VIRTUE OF HUMAN BEINGS IS FITNESS TO LIVE TOGETHER AS EQUALS; CLAIMING NOTHING FOR THEMSELVES BUT WHAT THEY AS FREELY CONCEDE TO EVERYONE ELSE; REGARDING COMMAND OF ANY KIND AS AN EXCEPTIONAL NECESSITY, AND IN ALL CASES A TEMPORARY ONE.

JOHN STUART MILL,
THE SUBJECTION OF WOMAN

## PRAYING FOR PURPOSE

❝ **'These are the things you are to do: Speak the truth to each other, and render true and sound judgment in your courts; do not plot evil against your neighbor, and do not love to swear falsely. I hate all this,' declares the Lord.** ❞
ZECHARIAH 8:16-17 NIV

**Lord,**
It sure isn't always easy being a human being. Sometimes I know I take it all for granted, and sometimes I try to wish it all away. I'm sorry, Lord, for those times. From here on out I will try to appreciate all the aspects of my life—the good and easy and the bad and difficult. I know you've got a plan for me, and it's my job to keep working at life and listening for your direction.
**Amen**

27

# Put Air in the Tires, and Check the Oil

> " **The earth is the Lord's and all that is in it, the world, and those who live in it.** "
> **PSALM 24:1**

Few days in the life of any teenager compare with the sixteenth birthday. Not because you're "sweet sixteen." Let's face it, that's kind of embarrassing. What is so exciting about the sixteenth birthday can be summed up in two words: THE CAR! In most states and for most teenagers, this is the day when you can legally get your driver's license. Probably many high school sophomores miss first and second period on that birthday because they are at the DMV getting the little plastic card that says: You can drive. Welcome to the real world!

It doesn't matter that your voice may not have changed completely, you still sleep with a retainer and several stuffed animals, or you haven't lost the baby fat in your face. You can drive, and the world better watch out! It doesn't matter that the car is a

## LET'S ASK STEVE!

Hey Steve,

I've got friends in my youth group who tell me the most important thing for me as a Christian is focusing on my inner walk with God, and I have friends at school who say that the most important thing is getting involved in causes that can save the world. Who is right? How should I prioritize things?

Caught in the Middle

Dear Caught,

That's a really good question. The reality is that *both* sets of friends make good points. God wants us to relate to him in a personal, committed, intimate way. At the same time, God is very concerned about how we relate to all of his world—the people around us as well as nature. I'd encourage you to think

of it like this: When you have a close friend, the closer and deeper your friendship becomes, the more you begin to understand and share your friend's concerns. It's the same way with God. The deeper your relationship to God and his Son, Jesus, becomes, the more you will find yourself caring about the things God values: people and all of creation!

Lord,

You have given us an incredible gift in this great, green earth. And I know that we haven't done such a terrific job of taking care of it. We've often gone about our business assuming that we'd never have to clean up, that nothing would ever run out. But now we're at a time when it looks like the earth is growing weak, and we must do everything we can to get her healthy again.

　　As I strive to live a worthy life in your light, I open myself to doing the very best I can do to take care of the earth. I ask for your direction in helping me to know where to focus and how best to help.

　　Each day I will try to live a "green" life, one where I reduce, reuse, and recycle. A life in balance with nature. I open myself to your guidance and thank you again for the incredible gifts of nature you have given us.

Amen

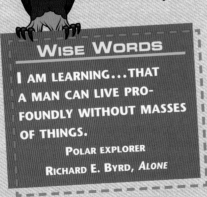

big ol' soccer-mom minivan or a station wagon with wood paneling. It has an engine, a steering wheel, and a driver's seat, and you're sitting in it! If you're over 16, you surely remember that first drive to school or to the store by yourself, with the radio playing, for years and years to come. If you haven't reached that day yet, I'll bet you have already pictured it in your head.

If you are anything like I was when I first got my license, that wood-paneled station wagon quickly becomes your home away from home. Half a dozen candy wrappers here, a few soda cans there, and some mildewing gym clothes in the back seat make up the décor. For me, the

gas gauge was perpetually close to empty. And checking the oil? I didn't know you could do that. Put simply, it is pretty easy to treat that first car as something to use at our whim, but we often neglect its care. We need to use gifts we truly value, but we also need to care for them.

The same principle holds true for our world. God has given humanity a wonderful gift beyond imagining in creation. There is creation's beauty, so spectacular that the art of van Gogh and Monet can't compare! Within the created world is everything we need to sustain ourselves. The air we breathe, the water we drink, the ground we till for food are all gifts and wonderful beyond belief.

Still, it's pretty easy for us to treat this gift like I treated

### BUMPER STICKER THEOLOGY

## EARTH: HANDLE WITH CARE. IT'S ONE OF A KIND!

that car in high school. Running it into the ground for my own enjoyment but not treating it with the care and respect it needed.

God has given us the world we live in, not only to treat as our personal playground but also to care for and treat with respect. One word often used for this responsibility is "stewardship." A steward is someone given care of an estate by the owner. A steward makes decisions about the estate's care on behalf of the owner.

We are God's stewards here on earth. We are the caretakers (think about that word, care-takers) of creation. We are free to enjoy and celebrate the world we live in, but at the same time it is up to us to care for God's created world. This responsibility is ours not only for our good (we need clean water to drink, air to breathe, fuel to feed our bodies) but also because the world isn't ours. It's God's. We have use of it, but it is God's creation that we either care for lovingly or abuse with neglect.

If we are serious about living purposeful lives, we'll be concerned with how our decisions impact the whole world. We have the opportunity to be leaders in our schools and communities—caretakers of the world we live in.

## THIS WEEK ON EARTH

It's cool to think about saving the rain forest or helping to combat global warming, but for this week, let's hit a bit closer to home. Come up with three ways you can lovingly care for the world around you. It could be anything!

1.

2.

3.

Reread your list every day this week to remind you of your commitment to be a good caretaker of God's world!

## PRAYING FOR PURPOSE

> **The Lord God took the man and put him in the garden of Eden to till it and keep it.**
> **GENESIS 2:15**

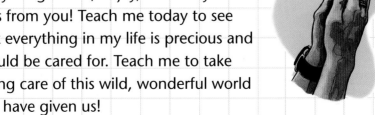

**Dear God,**
Thank you for this day! Thank you for everything I have, enjoy, use. They are all gifts from you! Teach me today to see that everything in my life is precious and should be cared for. Teach me to take loving care of this wild, wonderful world you have given us!
**Amen**

# What Do the Grand Canyon and a Hot Fudge Sundae Have in Common?

> " The heavens are telling the glory of God; and the firmament proclaims his handiwork. "
> **PSALM 19:1**

What *do* the Grand Canyon and a hot fudge sundae have in common? Or for that matter, the Pacific Ocean and the human eye? "Hey," they shout to us, "look at what

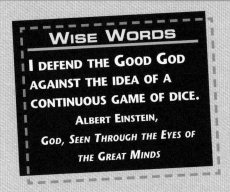

awesome stuff God has made!" Even better, they show that God is saying to us, "Not only is this stuff amazing, but I made it all for you!" It doesn't really matter what you like. Are you thrilled by huge, powerful things? Well, take a look at the Himalayas, redwood trees, or a blue whale. Are you fascinated by detail? Check out the intricate design of a snowflake or the human nervous system.

You're a tough, macho guy's kind of guy? Observe the force of a hurricane or the athleticism of a cheetah or the sheer power of a great white shark. More of the sensitive type? How about the softness of a kitten or the fragile beauty of a tulip?

It's as if your folks dropped you off at the mall, handed you the family credit card, and said, "The sky's the limit. You can have anything you like." As awesome as each beautiful sunset is, the best part is

## LET'S ASK STEVE!

Hey Steve,
Some of the kids in school say it's impossible to believe in God and to believe in science at the same time. Is this true?
Baffled in Biology

Dear Baffled,

I don't believe you have to pick one or the other. Some of the great scientific minds of history, Albert Einstein for one, and many scientists today believe that the amazing intricacy of the scientific or natural world suggests that there must be a God behind it all. Personally, I'd ask, "If the world is ruled by laws of science or principles that never change and happen over and over, year upon year upon year, doesn't that suggest that maybe some larger power set those principles in motion?" To me that makes more sense than thinking everything is just one big accident. So, I'd say the more science you know, the more remarkable God becomes.

that the sun comes up the next morning, and it all starts over! And it's free. You can't make it to the Great Barrier Reef in Australia today or visit the Rocky Mountains? It doesn't matter. Just take a moment and watch how your hand functions. Look at the way the light comes through the dirt on the window in your geometry class. (A note of caution: Don't look too closely for the wonder of God's creation in that casserole they serve in the school lunchroom. That might be pushing it!)

If you've gone to school for more than a week or two, you've heard that some people think nature tells us that the world has evolved over time and others think God created the universe in a moment. I'd argue that it doesn't matter.

### GOD IS AMAZING!

What's the most amazing thing you saw in the natural world today? A Barry Bonds home run? The cute guy in English class? A rose? Your brother actually doing his share of the dishes?

Take a few minutes every day this week to write down a few of the things around you that are truly amazing. Commit yourself to being aware of all God's good gifts to you!

**Father in heaven,**
Make me worthy of experiencing all the incredible miracles and blessings you create and give us each and every day. This life you have given is such an incredible gift, and I know sometimes I take it for granted. Sometimes I complain and forget about all the miracles that are happening every moment all around me.

I pray that you will guide me each day to appreciate your gifts. And I pray that I might learn to live in such a way that I am valuable in helping others to also be thankful for the awesome creations you have shared. This I pray with my whole heart, in your name,
**Amen**

C. S. Lewis, one of the great Christian writers of the 20th century, made the argument that even evolution speaks to the wonder of a creating God. He felt that if evolution is the way God chose to bring things about, it would still be utterly amazing. How else do you explain starting with an amoeba swimming in some soup a million years ago and ending up with Michael Jordan and Beyoncé a million years later? He would say that whether God made the world in an instant or gradually over millions of years, the intricacy and beauty of creation still makes us shake our heads in awe at God's goodness and creativity.

The trick for us is noticing. How awesome would it be if we even noticed one-tenth of the phenomenal things God puts right in front of us every single day? If we really noticed just how great pizza is? Or that our brains can have us talk on the phone, watch TV, and do homework all at the same time?

I encourage you to look around today and notice three wonderfully wild things about the natural world that God has made that you've never really paid attention to before. Have fun!

## AMAZING STUFF

Are there days when you just can't think of anything to be thankful for? We all have them. Those blue times when you just want to look heavenward and shout, "Why me, God? Why does everything bad happen to me?"

Well, here's a little trick to help pull you out of the pits when you start to sink. Start a list. Not just any list. This is going to be a list you add to every day. So you'll need a really HUGE piece of paper. You might want to get a special notebook—or maybe a clipboard with a stack of paper—something you can keep adding to and adding to.

### BUMPER STICKER THEOLOGY

**LIKE THE SUNSET? CHECK OUT THE ARTIST WHO PAINTED THE SKY!**

Every night, before bed, add at least one thing. What are you putting on the list? Add stuff that God created that is absolutely awesome. Could be your cat. A pickle. The smell of freshly baked bread. Got the idea?

Then, when you think God hasn't done anything for you lately, pull out the list. You'll be amazed!

## *YOUR TURN!*

God does amazing stuff! And who is it for? Well, it's for you. And me. For his children. For all of us.

And do we create anything amazing for him? Think about it. Did you make someone smile today? Did you help a friend stay away from a party where there were drugs? Did you snuggle with your kitty? Help an older woman from your church learn to use her e-mail?

There are a million and one ways we can create amazing stuff for him here on earth. Write down five things you've created this week:

1.

2.

3.

4.

5.

Can you keep going?

# PRAYING FOR PURPOSE

> "When I look at your heavens, the work of your fingers, the moon and the stars that you have established; what are human beings that you are mindful of them, mortals that you care for them? Yet you have made them a little lower than God, and crowned them with glory and honor. You have given them dominion over the works of your hands; you have put all things under their feet."
>
> **PSALM 8:3-6**

**Dear God,**

Wow! There's so much all around me that points to your power and awesomeness. Thank you for even making it possible for me to see, hear, taste, and touch this beautiful world of yours. Help me be aware of what you put in front of me every day. Help me notice your goodness and artistry in even the commonplace things around me. Finally, help me be grateful for the beauty and wonder of this day and every day to come!

**Amen**

# Every Sunset Is
# an Instant Message
# from God

Why is it we can sit in physics class and be completely
baffled by the concepts and formulas up on the
board, but then we go to baseball practice and put
the same concepts into play with hardly a second
thought? Or, why can it be so confusing to be in a
political science class and discuss the theories of

justice, liberty, oppression, and imperialism, but after renting and watching *Braveheart,* it all makes perfect sense? The reason is that we are drawn to the practi-

Hey Steve,

I'm sitting in church, looking out at the beautiful sunny day. Do I really need to be here? Why can't I learn all I need to know about God and worship him outside in his creation?

Got Spring Fever

Dear GSF,

You are certainly right that you can learn a great deal about God and be thankful to him as you walk around and observe the beauty of creation. Whether it's a beautiful sunset; the intricacy of a snowflake; the clockwork-precise rhythm of the planets, moon, and stars; or the complexity of your own body, God's creation shows us so many things about God. It is a great idea to learn all you can from creation and to be thankful to God for everything you see, hear, touch, feel, and taste.

At the same time, there's more to learning about God and worshiping him than what you can do in the great outdoors. Theologians call nature God's general revelation, or things he shows to all of us in general ways. They have a term called special revelation for things like the teachings of the Bible, the stories in Scripture of God's interactions with people through history. That's what we learn in church. We also need church to connect to, learn from, and celebrate with others who love God.

So, keep going to church and look for signs of God there, but absolutely keep looking for God's messages to you in the created world you see every day.

cal. We respond to the lessons we can see in front of us. Some people call it hands-on experience, but whatever you call it, the fact is most of us learn more easily by doing or seeing than by sitting and thinking. That's how God wired us.

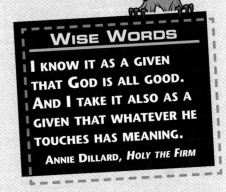

If that is how God made us, it would make sense that he'd give us lessons to observe and learn from in the world around us. Let's take a minute and see if we can't find a few.

A couple lessons from God's created world are mentioned in the Bible. In Matthew 6, Jesus uses the examples of birds and lilies to show us that if God cares for every bird that flies and every flower that grows, he certainly cares for each of us. In Proverbs 6, the writer uses the ant as an example of how working diligently in good times can pay off when times get rough. Those are examples where the Bible specifically teaches us about creation; maybe we can draw some lessons of our own.

Something as massive as our solar system teaches us a very specific and personal lesson about God's love for us. Look at the earth's position relative to the sun. We are thousands upon thousands of miles from the sun, yet if things were just 1 percent different it would have a disastrous effect on us. If we were even 1 percent closer to the sun, the heat would burn off our atmosphere and boil our oceans. If we were 1 percent farther away, everything would freeze and life would be impossible. The earth is the exact distance from the sun for the conditions we need for our existence to be possible. What a great example of God's care for us!

Each cell of our body is a lesson in our importance to God. In the natural world, cells look pretty much alike. A tree cell isn't that much different from the cell of a slug, which in turn isn't much different from a skin cell of Orlando Bloom. Yet, in spite of how similar every living cell is, each human cell is the perfect combination of DNA to put together a person. With just a few variations, people have the genetic material to be able to compose symphonies, paint the *Mona Lisa,* and throw curveballs. The particular detail of the makeup of each cell of our bodies tells us how significant we are to God.

What does this have to say about living a life of purpose? Tons! If God values you enough to go to such great and specific care in putting you together, your life matters. Sometimes we question our importance or value. If we really understand the great care God took in our creation, we'd quickly banish those thoughts to the ridiculous part of our brain!

Additionally, the lives of the people around you matter. There's no such thing as a "dorky little brother" or a "nerdy kid" in the locker next to yours or a "boring, good-for-nothing" teacher. Everyone you

**BUMPER STICKER THEOLOGY**

**CREATION: GOD'S CLASSROOM**

44

meet is someone God went to great care to create. That person, and every other person, is someone you should value and respect. After all, God does!

## LESSONS ON THE FLY

What to you is the height of human beauty? A LeBron James dunk, a Michelle Kwan triple toe loop, a Dave Matthews song? What does it teach you about God?

Take a minute to observe your hand. Move your fingers. Point. Pick something up. Consider how quickly your hand takes your mind's thought and puts it to action. What does your hand teach you about God?

Grab your favorite food. Perhaps it's ice cream or an orange or fries. Notice all the sensations you experience as you eat. Think about what your body does to turn the food into energy. Consider how your mouth can distinguish from hundreds of different tastes to recognize this, your favorite food. What does all this teach you abut God?

## IT'S ALL GIBBERISH ... OR IS IT?

Sometimes it seems God speaks to us in code or metaphor. Sometimes we get it, but maybe sometimes we don't. Just for fun, try this and see if you can "get" the message:

Get together with a friend, and take turns trying to explain to each other how to do something.

Only the catch is . . . you can't use English. (Or any other real language.) You have to use gibberish! (Everyone speaks fluent gibberish, right?) You can also gesture, but you can't use real words. See how long it takes you to figure out what the message is.

The next time you're trying to figure out what God is saying, remember to *really* look and *really* listen. You'll get the message eventually!

## Brought to You by . . . GOD!

Do you watch television? (It's okay, almost all of us do!) What kinds of shows do you watch?

Get together with a few friends and consider the following:

• What if God were the proud sponsor of a television show? What would that show be about? What would it teach? What would the commercials be about?

• What do you think God thinks about prime-time television?

## What Message Is God Trying to Send Through You?

This is another way of asking yourself these questions: Where am I going? What am I doing? What is the meaning of my life?

Find a quiet place to relax where you know you won't be disturbed. Get comfortable, and close your eyes. Imagine you are checking your e-mail. You look in your inbox, and there is a note from God!

Open the e-mail. Read it. Slowly. Carefully. What is God telling you? What is God asking you? How do you answer?

## PRAYING FOR PURPOSE

**"You knit me together in my mother's womb. I praise you, for I am fearfully and wonderfully made. Wonderful are your works. "**
**PSALM 139:13-14**

**Heavenly Father,**
I want to tell you that I am listening. This time I'm not asking anything of you. I'm not asking anything from you. I just want you to know that I am here. I am trying with all my might to live a life that both you and I can be proud of. And I am listening. I pray with all my heart that I might hear and understand your message. I pray that I might know which way to turn at every bend of the path. And so I pause today, and I will pause every day. To listen to your words, to your guidance, to your wisdom. I love you, Father.
**Amen**

# WHAT JESUS DOES FOR US

" [Jesus] existed before everything else began, and he holds all creation together. "

**COLOSSIANS 1:17 NLT**

Why has Jesus been the most written about, talked about, and followed person in the last 2,000 years of world history? Just because he was a great teacher? He was that, but he was also much, much more. His was the most important life ever lived. This collection of essays looks at what the Bible has to say about who exactly Jesus was and what he does for us so many years after he lived on earth!

# Jesus Is God's Beloved Son

**"** **As Jesus was coming up out of the water, he saw heaven being torn open and the Spirit descending on him like a dove. And a voice came from heaven: 'You are my Son, whom I love; with you I am well pleased.'** **"**
**MARK 1:10–11 NIV**

Our identity, who we believe we are, is very important. Who we are dictates the things we do and where we'll go in life. Think about it: If you believe you're an intelligent student with an aptitude for science, chances are you'll get good grades in science class. If you're always hitting jumpers on the court in your driveway, you'll probably try out for the basketball team. Likewise, if people tell you you're stupid and ugly, you may come to believe them. You'll *feel* stupid and ugly. Pretty soon, you'll feel depressed and stop caring about how well you do in school.

See how important our identity is? It drives our behavior and defines who we are. To further prove the point, take a look around your school at all the different cliques: the brains, the jocks, the mathletes, and the cheerleaders. Each group has its own identity, and each behaves quite differently. The brains are busy studying, the jocks are pumping iron, the math-letes are fiddling with their calculators, the cheer-leaders... well, they're popular.

Jesus' identity is that he is the Son of God. He's not just any son—Jesus is the *beloved* Son of God. Everything he says and does is because of his relationship with his Father. Jesus teaches with authority on the Scriptures, and he has the power to heal the sick and raise the dead—because of who he is.

Jesus finds the strength to resist Satan's temptations in the desert because Jesus remembers who he is (Matthew 4:1-11). Jesus doesn't fall into Satan's trap because he knows, as the beloved Son of God, what he came to earth to do. He knows that Satan's way isn't God's way.

## FIND YOUR PLACE IN THE SON!

Jesus found courage to die on the cross because he knew—despite how awful it would be—that he, as the Son of God, had come to die for us. Jesus knew that he would be raised from the dead and go back to heaven to be with his Father.

Even from an early age, Jesus knew who he was. Each year Jesus' family and relatives made the long trek to Jerusalem for the Passover Feast. One year, when his family was returning home, 12-year-old Jesus decided to stay behind in the temple and hang out with the rabbis so he could talk about the Scriptures with them (Luke 2:41–50). The rabbis were amazed at how much the young boy understood. Three days later a frantic Mary and Joseph finally found him back at the temple. When they told him how worried they had been and asked him how he could do that to them, he answered, "Why were you searching for me? Did you not know that I must be in my Father's house?"

Mary and Joseph didn't completely understand what it meant that Jesus was the Son of God—but Jesus knew. And he lived every moment of his life by his special identity as the beloved Son of God.

Do you know that you have a special identity, too? (And it's not brain, jock, mathlete, cheerleader, stupid, or ugly.) Because Jesus lived by his identity, you get a new one, too! If you have accepted by faith Jesus Christ as the one who saves you and leads you through life, then you share in his identity. You are a beloved child of God, too.

And just like Jesus, you no longer have to live up to the expectations of others. You don't have to feel the pressure to be something you're not.

Being a beloved child of God will not always be easy—just as it wasn't always easy for Jesus. But being God's child means you are always loved and will never be alone, even through the toughest times of your life. Now *that's* an identity worth living every day!

Jesus has a special name for you. When you became a child of God, you received a new name and a new identity. That's how Peter and Paul got their names—Jesus saw who they really were and what they could do for the Kingdom of God, and he gave them new identities.

You have a new name, too—a brand-new identity. This new name describes the core of who you are as God sees you. It's a special name—a term of endearment—that Jesus uses only for you!

## WHAT'S MY NAME?

The world does a lot to tell us we aren't worth much. So we start listening to this negative stuff and believe it's who we really are. We name ourselves things like stupid, ugly, average, unimportant, overweight, etc. But Jesus won't stand for that! He's all about changing our names; he has a special one just for you. Take some time to be alone with Jesus, and let him tell you his new name for you.

**Step 1:** Grab a pen and paper, and write your first name in the center of the paper.

**Step 2:** Think about all the words that you think describe you, both the negative and the positive, and write those descriptive words all around your name. (But for every negative one you put down, you must put down a positive! It's fine to have more positives, though.)

**Step 3:** Pray and thank God for the positive things, and ask him to show you where you got the negative ones. This could take a while and it might be painful, but ask God to begin healing the hurt.

**Step 4:** Turn your paper over and ask God to tell you what your new name is. Then just listen for a while.

**Step 5:** Thank God for what he has revealed to you. And ask him to help you live out your new name.

## *PRAYING FOR PURPOSE*

" How great is the love the Father has lavished on us, that we should be called children of God!
And that is what we are! The reason the world does not know us is that it did not know him. "
**1 JOHN 3:1 NIV**

**Dear heavenly Father,**
Thank you for your beloved Son, Jesus. Thank you that I share in his identity. Help me live like I'm your beloved child. It's hard to do that when I'm having a hard day or when I make mistakes. When those days happen, help me remember your love and resist the temptation to think badly of myself. Remind me that  you're always there to comfort me, forgive me, and guide me. In Jesus' name,
**Amen**

# The True Face
# of God

" Philip said to him, 'Lord, show us the Father, and we will be satisfied.' Jesus said to him, 'Have I been with you all this time, Philip, and you still do not know me? Whoever has seen me has seen the Father.' "

**JOHN 14:8-9**

When I was a sophomore in college, my faith was rocked. I started to doubt all the stuff I believed about God from the time I was little. I wasn't even sure if I really knew who God was anymore. And just like the disciple Philip, I was desperate to see the Father.

I remember praying one night as I lay on my bed, in the dark. I was crying. In my prayer I begged God to reveal himself so I could believe in him again: "If you're really God, then you can do anything. You could send an angel right now to tell me to stop doubting and to believe. You could let me hear your voice. You could send me an unmistakable

## PURPOSEFUL PONDERABLE

WHY DOES JOHN CALL JESUS "THE WORD"? WELL, WHEN YOU WANT TO COMMUNICATE WITH SOMEONE, YOU USE WORDS, RIGHT? WHEN JESUS WAS ON EARTH, HE WAS GOD'S MOUTHPIECE. JESUS ALWAYS EMPHASIZED THAT EVERYTHING HE SAID CAME FROM THE FATHER. SO JESUS IS THE ULTIMATE WORD OF GOD!

sign. Please, God, I want to believe. I don't know what I'll do without you. Please reveal to me who you really are." My prayer was so earnest that I thought for sure God would speak to me.

When I was done praying, I continued to lie in the dark crying. And I waited . . . and waited. But nothing happened. I heard no voice from heaven. No angel appeared to me. Depressed and tired from crying, I finally fell asleep.

It'd make a good story to say something magical happened the next day and I was filled with belief. But I wasn't. I continued to struggle. Some days I had faith. Other days I was full of questions. As I look back on that time, I'm grateful that God didn't send an angel or give me a heavenly vision. What he gave me instead was Jesus.

Desperate to find magical answers from heaven—and having received none—I found myself drawn to Jesus to know God better. Perhaps that night when I cried and prayed, Jesus whispered to my heart while I slept: "Have I been with you all this time, Jenny, and you still don't know who I am? If you've seen me, you've seen the Father."

Today when I struggle with my faith, I go to Jesus. Christian books have given me insight. Sermons have inspired me. Small group Bible

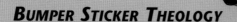

**BUMPER STICKER THEOLOGY**

**NO JESUS, NO GOD.
KNOW JESUS, KNOW GOD.**

studies have taught me new things. Each one has been valuable in helping me live the Christian life. But *nothing* and *no one* brings me closer to God than Jesus.

Do you ever wonder what God is really like? Look no farther than Jesus! The Bible tells us that Jesus is the image of the invisible God (Colossians 1:15). That means when we look at Jesus, we're really looking at God. Everything we know about God—his love, his goodness, his power, his authority (yup, everything!)—is found in Jesus.

God knew from the beginning that we would want to know (and need to know) what he's all about. And he wants to show you who he is, too! If you find yourself scratching your head at some point wondering what the deal is with God, remember that he's not playing hide-and-seek or trying to make knowing him difficult: All you have to do is look at Jesus. The Father sent us his Son—the image of the invisible God—so that we could know exactly what God is like.

## LEARN MORE

Check out these passages about Jesus to learn more about God:

1. God loves us (John 15:9–13)
2. God is all-powerful to help us (Luke 8:22–25)
3. God forgives all our sins (Matthew 9:2–8)

4. God gives us what we need (Matthew 14:13–21)
5. God defends us when we're weak (Luke 7:36–50)
6. God is patient with us (Mark 14:32–42)
7. God corrects us when we need it (Mark 10:35–45)
8. God is never too busy to be with us (Mark 10:13–16)

God took a huge step when he sent Jesus into the world. See, the Israelites knew God spoke to them through prophets such as Abraham and Moses and David. But more than anything, God wanted to get really, really close to us—to feel our pain, joys, and sorrows as a human being. So, Jesus left his heavenly throne to move into our crummy neighborhood just so he could show us first-hand what God is all about.

## *Do It!*

Here are ten ways you can be a living word of God to those around you:

1. **Help an elderly neighbor with house or yard work, and don't take any money.**
2. **Seek out a friend who's having a hard time, and ask how he or she is doing. Then really listen—without talking about yourself even once. Afterward ask if you can pray for and with that person.**
3. **Call a local food bank, and ask how you can volunteer to help. To make it extra fun, ask a friend to join you.**

4. Make an effort to be nice to someone who usually drives you crazy—even if it's your little brother or sister!
5. Refuse to talk about people behind their backs.
6. **Write a thank-you note to your favorite teacher.**
7. Talk to the quiet guy or girl in school who everyone ignores or makes fun of.
8. **Invite a non-Christian friend to go with you to church or youth group.**
9. Help your youth leader clean up after an event.
10. **Look into sponsoring a child. You could sponsor on your own or ask your youth leader if your youth group, Sunday school class, or small group can sponsor a child together.**

## PRAYING FOR PURPOSE

> **So the Word became human and lived here on earth among us.**
> **JOHN 1:14 NLT**

**Dear God,**
Thank you for sending your Son, Jesus, to the world so we could know you better through him. I want others to know you, too. So help me share you with people by how I live and how I treat them. Like your Son, let me be a living word of God to those around me. In Jesus' name,
**Amen**

# Does Anybody Really Care?

Ever wonder if God cares? Have you questioned whether he just sits a million miles away up in heaven somewhere and doesn't know anything about what's going on in your life? Most of us have at some point. It can be hard to believe that a God who is all-powerful and bigger than the entire universe cares about whether or not I lose those ten pounds I've been worried about or whether you get the date to homecoming you've been hoping for all semester. Hard to believe? Maybe, until you stop to take

**God,**

Thank you for being the all-knowing, compassionate, and merciful God that you are. I work to be like you, but that compassionate part can sometimes be hard. I want to be able to be there for those who need a friend, to listen, to comfort, to help heal. Please help me do your work here on earth. Help me face difficult people. Give me the strength and courage to go beyond my petty prejudices to see the beauty in everyone.

My goal is to follow your teachings—to live a life that honors you. I ask for your help and guidance to keep learning how I can best serve and help. Thank you, God.

**Amen**

---

## WHAT'S MY STORY?

ALL OF US HAVE SOME STORY WE'RE DYING TO TELL, BUT WE WONDER IF ANYONE WOULD LISTEN. TAKE A FEW MINUTES AND JOT YOURS DOWN. A SITUATION WITH FRIENDS AT SCHOOL. ISSUES WITH EATING. GUILT OR SHAME FROM THE PAST. A BROKEN FAMILY. DON'T WORRY ABOUT HIDING OR HAVING THE RIGHT WORDS. JUST WRITE. GOD IS ANXIOUS TO HEAR FROM YOU.

---

a look at God's Son, Jesus. Here's a story from his life that might change your mind.

Things are really starting to break big for Jesus. He's been talking to people and has performed miracles. He's generated a lot of buzz. Crowds of people follow him everywhere he goes. Word is getting out. This Jesus guy, he's the real deal! And

Hey Steve,

My pastor says God loves all of us. I don't think he ever met me. I've got things in my past that are pretty ugly. Stuff I've done and stuff I've experienced that I'm really ashamed of. If God is good and pure, I'm sure he wouldn't want anything to do with someone as screwed up as me. Am I right?

Sure God Doesn't Like Me

Dear SGDLM,

I am excited to say you are wrong. Totally wrong! God cares especially for people like you. People with a past, people with skeletons in the closet, people who don't think anyone understands. In the Bible, in Titus, chapter 3, Paul describes the worst of us when he says "we ourselves were once foolish, disobedient, led astray, slaves to various passions and pleasures, passing our days in malice and envy...hating one another." But he goes on to say, "but when the goodness and loving kindness of God our Savior appeared, he saved us...but according to his mercy." That's true for me, and my friend, I'm very happy to say it's true for you!

now, here's a great opportunity. Jarius, one of the richest, most powerful men in town, has a sick daughter, and he wants Jesus to save the day. Word is out, and everyone in town is crowding around Jesus as he heads to Jarius's house. Jesus' closest friends can hardly believe their luck. You can't buy this kind of publicity. The streets are packed with everyone who's anyone, and when Jesus performs this miracle, his fame is going to shoot through the roof!

What nobody knows, or cares about, is that there's a woman in the crowd with a desperate plan of her own. She's not here to get in on the party at Jarius's. You see, this woman has problems of her own. She's had a disease that has caused her to bleed internally for more than a decade. She's tried everything, every doctor, every quack remedy. All she has to show for it is that she's completely broke, penniless. To make matters worse, in this culture, a disease like this designates a person as "unclean," and that means that no one, not even friends or family, are allowed to associate with, touch, or offer that person a hug of comfort. That's her situation. Sick with a disease that has sapped her health and energy, totally ruined financially, and without a friend or human relationship in the world.

As the Jesus caravan rolls through her part of town, she sneaks through the crowd. The crowd is so thick she can barely move, and she has to struggle to even keep track of where Jesus is. She's persistent, though, and she works her way toward him. She has no intention of asking for his help. *Come on! Jesus is on his way to Jarius's house. He's on the A-list. They don't even make lists for people like me,* she thinks. She's not going to even talk to him, just touch his clothes when he walks by. That's the best she can hope for; maybe some good will come from that.

She touches his clothes, and chaos breaks out. Jesus comes to a screeching halt. The surging, rushing crowd backs up like a 20-car pileup on the highway. Jesus wants to know who touched him. His friends can't believe it! "Are you kidding, Jesus, there's hundreds of people here and dozens bumping up against you." He's serious, though; he wants to know.

So she tells him. "It was me." But, she doesn't stop there. She then says words we all need to say to God. She "told him the whole truth." She tells him about the sleepless nights, the string of doctors that do no good but take her money anyway. She tells him about the loneliness. This is not a short story.

The crowd is antsy. Jesus' friends are furious. They want to get on to the big stuff! Jarius is impor-

> ### TRY THIS
>
> IS THERE ONE THING THAT YOU THINK KEEPS YOU APART FROM GOD? OR APART FROM BEING AS CLOSE AS YOU WISH TO BE? GO INTO THE BATHROOM OR YOUR BEDROOM—A PLACE WHERE YOU CAN BE ALONE—AND LOOK INTO A MIRROR. LOOK INTO YOUR OWN EYES, AND SAY: "GOD LOVES ME FOR WHO I AM. GOD HEARS MY PRAYERS. ALWAYS." DO THIS EVERY DAY THIS WEEK.

## WONDER IF GOD CARES?
## JESUS DIED TO PROVE HE DOES!

tant. He's got connections. This is what the crowd came to see. Not Jesus sitting down beside the road listening to some poor homeless nobody and her pathetic story. That's what they think. It might even be what we would think, but it's not what Jesus thought. You see, he cares for this woman the way God cares for each of us. He wants to hear every word.

The woman walked away doubly healed that day. Her disease was gone but so was her loneliness. Jesus did eventually get to Jarius's house, and he performed an amazing miracle there, too. One final thing happened beside that road that day. Jesus sent a message to each of us. Still wonder if God cares? Still wonder if he notices?

## OPEN YOUR HEART

Who is it that totally gives you the creeps? Street people? The homeless? The developmentally disabled? The strange guy who sits behind you in science? Is there someone you just think is icky? It's okay. Really. We all have thoughts like that.

The task is to approach that person. It doesn't have to be any big thing. Just approach him or her. Say hello. Be warm and open. Listen to the inner voice that tells you what is right. Welcome that person into your heart.

That's what Jesus would do.

## PRAYING FOR PURPOSE

> " **For God so loved the world that he gave his only Son, so that everyone who believes in him may not perish but may have eternal life.** "
> JOHN 3:16

**Dear God,**
Sometimes I really struggle to believe. I struggle to believe that you care. I struggle with my faith that you even exist. There are parts of my life, parts of my past, parts of what's going on today that I don't believe anyone would want to see. Things that would make people see me as "unclean," just like the woman who went to see Jesus. You cared for her. You listened to her. You healed her, not because of what she could do for you, but because that's what you do. You love people. Please, would you listen to my story, the whole thing? Would you heal me? Love me? Thank you.
**Amen**

# Jesus Prays for His Followers

" I pray for them. I am not praying for the world, but for those you have given me, for they are yours. "
JOHN 17:9 NIV

My friend Janelle was telling me about some struggles she was having. "What's the point of praying?" she had asked her youth pastor. "Jesus doesn't know I exist. I'm just this girl who always has everything go wrong. He's not listening! Sure, he cares about the world and all that stuff, but he doesn't care about me *personally.* My life can just fall apart, and it isn't going to make one speck of difference!"

I know I've felt the same way Janelle was feeling. Have you? Sometimes it seems too unbelievable to think that Jesus cares what happens to one insignificant teenager. The thing is that he *does* care. And not only that, he prays for us.

How do I know? Well, it's not like I got an

**BIBLE BITS & BYTES**

O Lord God of heaven, the great and awesome God who keeps covenant and steadfast love with those who love him and keep his commandments; let your ear be attentive and your eyes open to hear the prayer of your servant that I now pray before you day and night.
NEHEMIAH 1:5–6

e-mail from him or anything. Then again, maybe it is sort of like that. Come on. Think about it. Think about your life. There was one day for me, last week, when everything was going wrong. And I mean *wrong.* I failed an English test. (The first time in my entire life I

## LET'S ASK JENNY!

Dear Jenny,

My best friend, Becka, isn't Christian, and I'm worried about her. It isn't like she's a bad person or isn't religious. Her family is very observant, but her background is a different religion. It's just that I know that Jesus prays for his followers, so I don't think he'd pray for Becka. I love being best friends, and I don't want that to ever change. What should I do?

A Concerned Believer

Dear Concerned,

First off, it's great that you care so much for your friend. It's cool to know all different kinds of people from a variety of religious and ethnic backgrounds. The thing to remember is that there are lots of points of view. You know what's best for you and what

you believe, and that is really an incredible thing! Jesus prays for you! And what's important for Becka and for everyone is that they live a life of kindness and goodness and are true to their own beliefs. So you can go on being best buds with Becka and still keep your own faith strong. Respecting and honoring differences as well as similarities is a big part of a mature friendship. And don't forget, God loves each and every one of his creatures—that includes Becka and her family!

failed a test!) When I got home, I found out I was grounded for something my little sister did, which she blamed on me! Between all

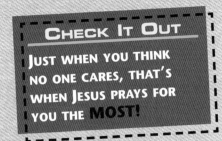
CHECK IT OUT

JUST WHEN YOU THINK NO ONE CARES, THAT'S WHEN JESUS PRAYS FOR YOU THE MOST!

that, my backpack split a seam and all my pens and pencils ended up on the gym floor. Of course I got in trouble for *throwing* them! And those were just the BIG things! My locker door jammed, and the girl I like happened to walk by when I was making this ridiculously stupid face at my best friend. But then, as I was walking to the library (I needed to ace the next English test, after all!), *I got it.*

I got the e-mail from Jesus. It was still March and pretty cold, and I was looking down as I walked. There, beside the sidewalk, was a flower. Sounds stupid, doesn't it? I mean, I'm not the kind of guy who goes around looking at flowers (not unless I'm buying

WE ARE SO LUCKY TO HAVE JESUS PRAY FOR US. REMIND YOURSELF EVERY DAY THAT HE IS WITH YOU. IT WILL KEEP YOU ON THE RIGHT PATH.

**P** RAISE HIM

**R** EMEMBER HIM

**A** LWAYS BELIEVE IN HIM

**Y** OU ARE LOVED BY HIM, DEEPLY AND COMPLETELY

**Jesus,**

It's so amazing to think that you are actually praying for me. Wow! I just don't really know quite what to say about that. That is so cool. I mean, me? Sometimes I don't think I'm worth it. I guess the main thing is that I want to always remember to keep you at the center of my life. I want to live as you lived—a life of goodness and right. And I want to always be worthy of your prayers.

Thank you, Jesus, for praying for me and for believing in me. I believe in you with all my heart.
**Amen**

a corsage for a dance!). But I really noticed this flower. It wasn't supposed to be there. No other flowers had bloomed yet. At first I just walked by. Then it hit me. *A flower.* It was a message. A sign. An e-mail!

It shook me up. It reminded me that Jesus was paying attention. That he *cared,* you know. And so I prayed as I walked the rest of the way to the library. I thanked the Lord for reminding me life wasn't so bad, and I prayed that things would get better in my life— and that I would always notice the flowers.

And you want to know the most totally awesome thing about all of this? I mean, think about it. If Jesus is praying for you—which he is—there isn't anything you can't accomplish!

# MEDITATION

Find a time and place where you won't be disturbed for at least 15 minutes. Sit in a comfortable position. Read over this medita-tion, and then close your eyes. If your thoughts wander, give some thought to the subject matter. It may pertain to the topic in some way you hadn't thought about. The mind can be

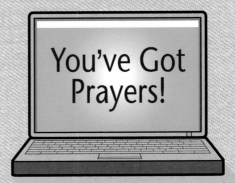

clever when it's trying to tell us something. Then gently remind yourself to get back on track.

*Imagine yourself outdoors in a beautiful setting. Look beside you and see a man. He is deep in prayer; he is praying for you. Silently let him know how much you appreciate his prayers. Let him know all that you wish he would pray for you. Don't be shy; he is there for you.*

Feel the power of his prayer. Think how it will impact your life. Realize how much you deserve his prayer. Allow yourself to sit there with him for as long as you wish.

When you are ready, open your eyes. You may feel calm, relaxed, and refreshed. Return to that setting with him whenever you wish.

## BUMPER STICKER THEOLOGY

### HONK IF JESUS PRAYS FOR YOU!

## LIST IT!

Jesus prays for me! Here are five things I can do for Jesus this week:

1.
2.
3.
4.
5.

## PRAYING FOR PURPOSE

> **Some children were brought to Jesus so he could lay his hands on them and pray for them....And he put his hands on their heads and blessed them before he left.**
> **MATTHEW 19:13–15 NLT**

**Dear Lord,**

Help me, I pray, to always remember that you are pulling me through, no matter what. When I start to feel down or stumble, remind me that I need to get back on track right away. Help me to be filled with the goodness of your prayers so that I may send you my praises and live according to your plan for me. And help me, please, Lord, to accept your prayers for me and allow your love to enter every part of my life. In Jesus' name, I pray.

**Amen**

# Your Good Shepherd

" I am the good shepherd. I know
my own and my own know me,
just as the Father knows me
and I know the Father. And I lay
down my life for the sheep. "
JOHN 10:14–15

If Jesus compares us to sheep, it's probably helpful to
know something about them, right? So here are some
interesting facts about sheep: Sheep are helpless. If
they fall over on their backs, they can't get back on
their feet. If they lay there too long, a wolf could
come along and tear them apart. Sheep are prone to
wander from the protection of the flock and get
lost—and a lone sheep is a dead sheep! Sheep are

dumber than dogs. Think about it: You can't train a sheep to sit, stay, or fetch a stick. No matter how hard you try, a sheep will never outwit Fido. In short, sheep need a shepherd—someone to carefully watch over them—or they're goners!

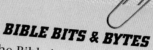

Whether we like it or not, we are very much like the sheep I just described. We are helpless to save ourselves. We are prone to wander from God and get lost. And while we have the highest intelligence of any creature in the food chain, we are surprisingly hard to train in the ways of God. Not a flattering picture, huh? But there is some very good news for us sheep.

Jesus is our good shepherd. A good shepherd loves his sheep. He is careful and watches to keep them from harm. The good shepherd will single-handedly fight off a wolf before he allows it to eat one of his sheep. A good shepherd *knows* and recognizes each sheep individually, so he *knows* when one has wandered off. And the Bible tells us that the good shepherd leaves the 99 sheep that are safely

## WRITE IT DOWN!

HOW MUCH DO YOU TRUST GOD? A LOT? A LITTLE? OR SOMEWHERE IN BETWEEN?

A: _ _ _ _ _ _ _ _ _ _ _ _ _ _ _ _

_ _ _ _ _ _ _ _ _ _ _ _ _ _ _ _ _

HOW WOULD YOUR LIFE BE DIFFERENT IF YOU RELIED ON JESUS MORE THAN YOU DO NOW?

A: _ _ _ _ _ _ _ _ _ _ _ _ _ _ _

_ _ _ _ _ _ _ _ _ _ _ _ _ _ _ _ _

together just so he can go after the one sheep that wandered off and is in danger (Matthew 18:12–14).

Being called sheep packs a hard punch to our fragile egos. But it's a very important reminder that God values us not because we are smart, successful, good-looking, or highly capable. The good shepherd loves and cares for us simply because we belong to him. Do you trust in Jesus to be your good shepherd? Or are you trying to make life work all on your own?

One more important thing about sheep: They know the voice of their shepherd. Back in biblical times, several shepherds would keep their flocks together in one big pen. When it was time for a shepherd to lead his flock to pasture, that shepherd would call his sheep — and only his sheep would leave the pen with him. The sheep belonging to the other shepherds stayed put. They would not go anywhere unless they recognized the voice of their own shepherd calling them.

## PURPOSEFUL PONDERABLE

THE PEOPLE OF ISRAEL DID NOT ALWAYS MAKE GOOD SHEEP. THEY WERE ALWAYS TRYING TO HELP THEMSELVES INSTEAD OF RELYING ON GOD TO BE THEIR SHEPHERD. GOD TOLD THEM THAT ONLY WHEN THEY WERE DEPENDENT ON GOD WOULD THEY EVER BE STRONG. ONLY WHEN THEY HUMBLED THEMSELVES AND TRUSTED HIM WOULD THEIR PLANS SUCCEED.

Sheep are so dependent on their shepherd that his is the only voice they know and trust. Amazing, huh?

When Jesus calls you today, do you notice? Do you recognize his voice? When he gives you direction for your life, do you know it is Jesus speaking? If not, perhaps you need to spend more time being a dependent sheep. When things get tough and you don't see a way through, rely on God to help you. When you notice that you've wandered away from him, remember that he's looking for you and wants you back. When you are struggling to be a better Christian and you can't seem to get it right, remember that God is patient and will be faithful to complete the good work he started in you. And after a while, you—just like those sheep—will know the voice of your good shepherd.

## *TAKE INVENTORY*

Step 1: Find a pen and a piece of paper.

Step 2: Ask Jesus to show you areas in your life that you have trouble trusting him with.

Step 3: Be still, and listen for God to reveal those areas to you. Write them down, and hang on to the paper so you can go back to it when you need to.

Step 4: End in prayer, asking God to help you trust him with every area of your life and to help you give him those things you want to do all by yourself.

## *PURPOSEFUL PRAYER*

**Dear Jesus,**

It's so easy to try and live my life on my own. But whenever I do that, things seem to fall apart on me. You'd think I'd learn by now to trust you more. But sometimes I still wonder if you really will come through for me. I worry that if I trust you to help me, you might forget about me. Maybe I don't really believe all the time that you are a *good* shepherd. Forgive me for that, and help me believe it. I know in my head that it's true, but my heart sometimes has a hard time catching up with what my head knows. Thanks for all your patience. I really do need you, Jesus, to take care of me. And I want to learn to hear your voice. Please teach me. In your loving name I pray,
**Amen**

# What Are You Training For?

" Do you not know that in a race
the runners all compete, but
only one receives the prize? Run
in such a way that you may win
it. Athletes exercise self-control
in all things; they do it to
receive a perishable wreath, but
we an imperishable one. "
1 CORINTHIANS 9:24-25

Every four years the Olympics come around, and the whole world notices hundreds of fabulously talented athletes. From gymnastics to water polo, from basket-ball to the marathon, we normal people watch in awe the exploits of these incredibly graceful and powerful athletes. A lot of us proba-bly fantasize about what it would be like to be them. We dream about what it would be like to have the speed of a gazelle, the grace of a swan, or the power of a lion. World-class athletes don't seem to be human like the rest of us!

## WISE WORDS

MANY PEOPLE HAVE THE
DESIRE TO WIN, BUT FEW
HAVE THE WILL TO PREPARE.
JUMA IKANGAA, FORMER BOSTON
MARATHON CHAMPION

The curious thing about the Olympics is that they are just a couple weeks long and, depending on the sport, feature each athlete for a matter of minutes, but it represents the work of a lifetime for each athlete. We see the seemingly effort-

less runner or the apparently calm and relaxed diver from the high dive. What we don't see are the hours upon hours of work that came before. We don't see them going to bed at eight on a Friday night because there is a big workout on Saturday morning. We don't see the athlete sitting at the fast-food joint drinking water while their friends stuff themselves with artery-clogging grease! We see the wonderful result. They live lives filled with self-discipline and hard work.

Living a purposeful life, a life following Jesus' example, is not that different. We want to be people who, when faced with the really tough choices, make the right ones. We want to be people who love and care for even the least lovely, most exasperating people. We want to be people who aren't swayed by

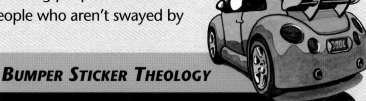

**BUMPER STICKER THEOLOGY**

**HOLY SWEAT: WORKING TODAY FOR GOD'S PLANS FOR TOMORROW.**

the crowd but who listen to God first and what he wants for our lives. But how do we become those kinds of people?

We need to make small, seemingly insignificant choices to be those kinds of people. A great runner doesn't wake up one morning and decide, "I think I'll go set the world record in the marathon today even though I haven't trained." She decides years in advance and makes thousands of small decisions that

## LET'S ASK STEVE!

Hey Steve,

I read verses in the Bible that talk about living a holy life and others that seem to give all kinds of rules for things to avoid and to do. Why is God so concerned with this stuff? Is he just out to make life boring and hard?

Just Want to Have Fun

Dear Fun,

You certainly aren't the first person to wonder if God is some kind of cosmic killjoy, sitting in heaven wanting to take away all our fun. I believe the opposite is the case. God wants you to have a rich, eventful, and significant life. He wants you to do and experience great things in your life of faith. To be ready to do this, every day you have to work on becoming a person who is prepared. Think of the spiritual and lifestyle disciplines that God asks you to have as spiritual sit-ups and push-ups. They may feel like a lot of work while you're doing them, but everyone loves to have the ripped abs when they show up at the beach in the summer!

move her toward that goal. Choices about getting out the door and training when the weather is bad, choices about going to bed when it would be more fun to play, choices to eat healthful foods when a triple bacon burger looks awfully good.

Well, the same principles apply in living a purposeful, God-pleasing life. Mother Teresa didn't wake up one morning and decide to become a saint. She decided God wanted her to serve people, so she started doing it, in tons of little ways every day. They added up. It works just like that for you and me. Every choice you make about how to spend your time on the Internet, or what to watch tonight on TV, or how to respond to that beer offered to you at last weekend's party is either moving you closer to or farther away from being the kind of follower Jesus needs to do his work in the world.

The difference between Olympic champions and really, really good athletes who got left at home often isn't natural-born talent. It usually is a difference in focus, a difference in self-discipline, a difference in purpose. Which kind of person do you want to be?

## DAILY TRAINING LOG

**Today's Workout**

What did I do today to consciously follow Jesus? What temptations did I resist? What service to others did I perform?

### Spiritual Caloric Input

How did I feed myself spiritually today? Time spent reading God's word? Time reading other Christian books? Time spent with youth group, church, other Christians?

### Conversation with Coach God

What time did I spend in prayer today? What did I talk to God about? What do I feel he is telling me?

## PURPOSEFUL PRAYER

**"While physical training is of some value, godliness is valuable in every way, holding promise for both the present life and the life to come. "**
**1 TIMOTHY 4:8**

**Dear God,**
I thank you today that you have great plans for my life. That you want me to follow you in ways that really make a difference. Help me have the courage to prepare myself to be ready for that kind of life. Help me make choices today that will shape me into a person "fit" for your service. Let me always remember to ask you, my heavenly coach, for advice on how to live my life.
**Amen**

# Jesus Laid Down His Life for You

> **For this reason the Father loves me, because I lay down my life in order to take it up again. No one takes it from me, but I lay it down of my own accord. I have power to lay it down, and I have power to take it up again. I have received this command from my Father.**
> JOHN 10:17–18

Nobody forced Jesus to die. He was free at any time to walk away from the cross. Satan tempted Jesus in the desert with that very fact. (Check out the tempta- tion story in Matthew 4:1–11.) In all three temp- tations Jesus faced in the desert, Satan basically says, "Look, Jesus, you don't have to do things the hard way. Give it up. Take the easy route. You can still

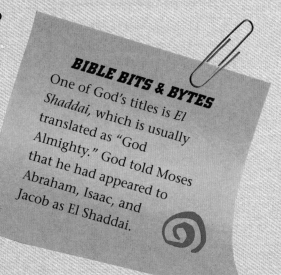

**BIBLE BITS & BYTES**
One of God's titles is El *Shaddai,* which is usually translated as "God Almighty." God told Moses that he had appeared to Abraham, Isaac, and Jacob as El Shaddai.

be a king if you do things my way." But Jesus refused to take the easy way out.

When Jesus was arrested in the Garden of Gethsemane, Simon Peter grabbed a sword and went after a guard, lopping off his ear. He did it to defend his best friend, Jesus. But Jesus set Peter straight: "Put away your sword….Don't you realize that I could ask my Father for thousands of angels to protect us, and he would send them instantly? But if I did, how would the Scriptures be fulfilled that describe what must happen now?" (Matthew 26: 52–54 NLT).

When Jesus hung on the cross, people harassed him, saying, "So! You can destroy the Temple and build it again in three days,

> ### THINK IT OVER!
> WE SHOULD BE WILLING TO LAY DOWN OUR LIVES FOR OTHERS JUST AS JESUS LAID DOWN HIS LIFE FOR US. WE DON'T HAVE TO DIE ON A CROSS FOR ANYBODY, BUT WE NEED TO LOVE PEOPLE UNSELFISHLY—PUTTING THEIR NEEDS BEFORE OUR OWN. WE CAN SAY WE LOVE OTHERS, BUT UNTIL WE TAKE ACTION TO LOVE THOSE AROUND US, THOSE WORDS DON'T MEAN SQUAT. SO, WHO NEEDS YOUR LOVE TODAY?

can you? Well then, if you are the Son of God, save yourself and come down from the cross!" (Matthew 27:40 NLT).

But Jesus didn't call the angels from heaven to battle for him. And he didn't feel the need to prove himself to the maddening crowd. He didn't budge from that cross. He laid down his life. He died...for you and for me.

It's hard to believe that someone would go through such torture of his own free will. Isn't that a little bit crazy? Maybe. But love drives us toward some pretty crazy things, doesn't it?

It was love that drove Jesus to make the choice that he did. It was his Father's will

*BUMPER STICKER THEOLOGY*

**JESUS ON THE CROSS: "I'D RATHER DIE THAN LIVE WITHOUT YOU."**

to save us and forgive us. The only way that could happen was for Jesus, the Sinless One, to die in our place. Jesus chose the cross out of love for his Father and his Father's will. But Jesus also did it because he loves *us.* Jesus said, "No one has greater love than this, to lay down one's life for one's friends" (John 15:13). There is no love better or greater than the love Jesus has for you. Your parents can't love you more. Your friends can't love you more. Even if you get married someday, your spouse won't love you more than Jesus loves you. And Jesus laid down his life to prove it.

Knowing that Jesus loves us that much ought to be life-changing. But sometimes we hear about Jesus' death and resurrection so often that we tune it out: "Jesus loves me this I know!" Yada, yada, yada. What else is new, right? And we go about our lives not living in the reality of his love. We worry about stuff instead of handing it over to God. We hide our secret sins because we think they're too big for God to forgive. We desperately try to find a place to belong in the world around us, and we forget that we already belong in the family of God!

Thankfully God is willing to remind us—often—of his love. If you're at a place where you aren't living in the truth of God's love for you, ask him to give you a fresh experience of it. Then wait, watch, and listen for his love. It might come to you in the stillness of the night just before you fall asleep, in the hug of your little sister, or during worship on Sunday. But watch for it. Listen for it. You might be surprised by how often God actually says, "I love you."

## WRITE IT DOWN!

**How does it make you feel to know that Jesus laid down his life for you?**

A:

**Has Jesus' love transformed your life? How? If not, why?**

A:

**Is it easy or hard for you to put others before yourself? To "lay down your life" for them? Why?**

A:

**Has anyone—other than Jesus—put your needs before their own? How did that act of love make you feel?**

A:

**What can you do to unselfishly love someone today?**

A:

> "We know love by this, that he laid down his life for us—and we ought to lay down our lives for one another. How does God's love abide in anyone who has the world's goods and sees a brother or sister in need and yet refuses to help? Little children, let us love, not in word or speech, but in truth and action."
>
> **1 JOHN 3:16-18**

**Dear Jesus,**

I'm amazed by how much you love me. You laid down your life for me! And nobody forced you to do it. I'll never be able to repay you for that. But I want to learn how to love others the way that you love me. Fill me with your love so I can give it away. In your name I pray,

**Amen**

# Jesus Cares for the Scared and Lonely

> ## He heals the brokenhearted, and binds up their wounds.
> ### PSALM 147:3

Does life just sometimes seem to get you down? Do you feel hopeless? Are you tempted with sins when you know you should turn away? Do drugs or alcohol ever seem like an easy way out of the bad feelings? Are you ever scared? Scared of violence at your school? Scared by what you hear on the news? Scared by what may be going on in your own home? Do you ever feel that you don't fit the stereotype of what's considered attractive by the media? Do you eat too much? Not enough? Binge? Purge? Are you sick of all these questions?

If you answered yes to any of the above (well, except maybe the last one!), then you really need to read on. And if you didn't answer yes to even one of those, just be sure you're being honest with yourself. In the unlikely event you can't answer yes to any of the questions, I'll bet you know someone who can. So read on. Here's the deal. It's no easy feat being a teenager these days.

**THOUGHT FOR THE WEEK**

WHENEVER I'M DOWN, JESUS LIFTS ME UP.

There is so much stuff to deal with, so many choices, so many nasty things that happen out in the world. It's not the same planet that your grand-parents and parents were raised in. There are many more dangers and temptations. The media keeps on getting more and more detailed at broadcasting an image of what we all should look like and how we should act and what we should do. In other words, we've got our hands full these days learning to love ourselves as Jesus loves us and avoiding more sins than our parents could've even imagined!

There is indeed much to fear in this crazy world we live in. But having faith in the Lord can make all the difference between cowering under the covers and letting God help us face each new challenge each day with courage, conviction, and strength. Often, all we need is to talk about this stuff. Talk about it in prayers. Share your concerns, your moods, and your fears. And talk about it with other

**BUMPER STICKER THEOLOGY**

**JESUS LOVES YOU—
SO YOU SHOULD LOVE YOU, TOO!**

people who care about you.
It's so easy to think that
we're the only ones who
are depressed or afraid or
tempted—but it's every-
one. And by talking
together, we can learn that
we're among friends and we
can help each other. Jesus will help you
find the right person to talk to. You can count on it.

In spite of our faith and our efforts, what happens sometimes, when all of this gets to be too
much, is that we take it out on ourselves. Some kids

LORD,
WHEN I'M FEELING BURDENED,
LIKE I JUST CAN'T TAKE ANY MORE,
PLEASE HELP ME TO REMEMBER
JUST WHAT I WAS PUT HERE FOR.
I'M ON THIS EARTH TO SERVE YOU
AND HELP ALL THOSE WHO NEED ME.
SO IF MY PROBLEMS ARE BLINDING,
PLEASE HELP ME TO TRULY SEE.
I KNOW YOU WILL LIGHT MY PATH
AND HELP SHOW ME THE WAY,
AND EVEN WHEN THE WORLD SEEMS
   DARK,
THERE WILL COME A BRIGHTER DAY.

JESUS SEES THE BEAUTY IN ALL OF US.
CAN YOU FIND THAT BEAUTY IN
YOURSELF AND IN YOUR NEIGHBORS?

withdraw into themselves, become depressed. Others act out, becoming violent to either themselves or others. Eating disorders sometimes surface in the constant battle to be pretty enough, or thin enough, or muscular enough. But through it all, what we have to remember every day, every moment, is that Jesus is there for us! We have to keep that thought central.

There is no shame in asking for help. Sometimes we can feel stuck in a pit so deep we can't hear God speaking to us—it doesn't mean that you're not being a good Christian. God is still there helping you. Jesus has put people in your life who can help. Find them, and ask for help. And if you know someone who seems to be stuck in that pit, don't be afraid to talk to an adult about what you see that person going through. If one person won't listen, talk to another, and another, and another until someone hears you.

Just remember, there is a light at the end of even the darkest tunnel. Jesus is that light. He believes in us and in our ability to pull through and make good decisions. And if he believes in us, shouldn't we believe in ourselves?

## LIST IT!

Try these ideas the next time you're feeling blue. Write down people who love you. We've included the first, most important name.

1. Jesus
2.
3.
4.
5.

## IMAGINE GOOD THINGS

Even when life doesn't look too good to you, there are good things out there that the Lord has in store for you. Try to imagine them. Close your eyes and picture a huge department store. There is a stack of packages. Go closer and look at them; they have your name written on the outside. These are all the good things that Jesus wants for you. They are waiting for you to find your way to them. Let him light your path, and the journey will be easy! Now imagine yourself opening the packages! What is in them?

**REMEMBER:** Jesus wants good things for you, and he believes in you.

## TRUE LOVE LIST

Every day this week, write down something special about yourself—a reason to love yourself. Feel free to ask for help from friends if you need to.

1.

2.

3.

4.

5.

6.

7.

Here are some ideas of what to do when you're feeling burdened. If there's a blank, think about what you might do and fill it in.

What to do when...

### You're down:
1. Pray.
2. Help someone else.
3.
4. Find his light within you, and move out of the darkness.

### You're tempted:
1. Walk away. Quickly!
2. Imagine tomorrow and how you will feel if you give in to temptation.
3.
4. Find his light within you, and move away from the temptation.

### You've sinned:
1. Deal with the consequences.
2. Ask Jesus for forgiveness.
3. Forgive yourself.
4. Find his light within you, and move on in the brightness of a new day of forgiveness.

## WHEN TO ASK FOR HELP

1. You're afraid you might hurt yourself.
2. You're afraid you might hurt someone else.
3. You can't seem to function and get your daily activities done.
4. You're doing something that you hide (binging, purging, drinking, drugs, etc.).
5. You feel that life is hopeless.
6. You're doing something illegal (drinking or drugs or ?).
7. You're doing something immoral.

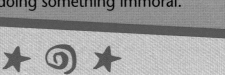

## WHO TO ASK FOR HELP

1. Parents
2. Pastor
3. Guidance counselor
4. Another relative
5. A friend you trust

# Praying for Purpose

God,

I think I really need to talk with you. I'm not doing very well right now. Life seems so compli- cated. And I'm just not handling it how I'd like.

Please help me take time to stop and catch my breath and listen to your advice. I know you are there for me. As long as I have faith and believe that you will guide me and lift my burdens, I can make it through this sad period. I'm going to try hard to keep moving in the right direction.

I really appreciate all your help and knowing that you're always there, and I'll try not to forget that. Please be patient with me, God, and help me see past my own burdens in order to live the life of faith and service that you have planned for me. In Jesus' name I pray,

Amen

# Do You Buy It?

Have you ever found something to be not quite what it claimed to be? The commercial was just so impressive. If you just buy one of these it will... give you a perfect smile, clear up your complexion, cause beautiful women to follow you everywhere you go, or bring excitement to every day. And then you buy it, and guess what? It's just toothpaste. You still get zits every few

days. Women pretty much pay the same amount of attention to you as they always did. That soda sold to you by all those skateboarding guys tastes good, but your day looks the same as before you drank it.

It's called hype. Sell. Making promises that aren't realistic. It doesn't just happen in marketing products for you to buy. Every movie ad you see tells you that this movie is going to be the most thrilling, inspiring, emotionally touching movie you'll see all summer—maybe in your entire life! SAT and ACT prep classes guarantee a tremendous test score that will get you into that elite college. Let's talk about that elite college for a second. "Don't go to

## FAITH COMMERCIAL

**TASK:** MAKE YOUR OWN COMMERCIAL FOR GOD
**TOOLS:** FAITH, CREATIVITY, VIDEO CAMERA

GET TOGETHER WITH A FRIEND OR TWO, AND MAKE A COMMERCIAL FOR SOMETHING THAT'S TOO GOOD TO BE TRUE BUT IS! MAKE A COMMERCIAL ABOUT YOUR FAITH. AFTER YOU'RE DONE, SHOW YOUR PASTOR AND SEE IF YOU CAN ARRANGE A SHOWING AT CHURCH!

## PURPOSE POINT

THE SECRET TO A PURPOSEFUL LIFE IS IN WHOM YOU FOLLOW. MILLIONS MARCHED AS FOLLOWERS OF CAESAR, NAPOLEON, HITLER. THESE WERE MEN WHO CLAIMED TO BE ALMOST GODS. NONE OF THEM LASTED.
WILL YOU LINE UP AS A FOLLOWER OF THE ONE MAN WHO CLAIMED TO BE GOD AND DELIVERED?

State U! If you really want your career to take off and your life to amount to anything, you've got to pay a gazillion dollars to come to Preppy U." Sure, it's an awesome school, but is it really going to be able to deliver the perfect future it promises? Or, "If you give yourself to our club soccer team, our football strength-training program, our weekly violin lessons, then we'll develop you into a big-time college athlete/musician." Maybe.

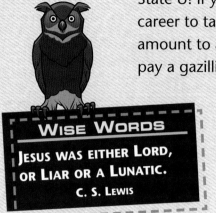

**WISE WORDS**

JESUS WAS EITHER LORD, OR LIAR OR A LUNATIC.
C. S. LEWIS

We're all trying to cut through hype. What's the real deal here? Your mom or dad have said it a million times: If it sounds too good to be true, it probably is.

Jesus made some pretty bold claims about himself. He said that getting to know him was as rewarding as finding water that would take away your thirst forever. He said that he was the ultimate expression of God's truth. He said that he was the way to have the fullest life possible. That's just the beginning.

So, what's with this guy? Was he incredibly full of himself and conceited? Maybe he was a little loopy. He could have just been a madman

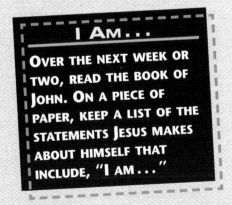

**I AM...**

OVER THE NEXT WEEK OR TWO, READ THE BOOK OF JOHN. ON A PIECE OF PAPER, KEEP A LIST OF THE STATEMENTS JESUS MAKES ABOUT HIMSELF THAT INCLUDE, "I AM..."

who thought he was all of those things but was really crazy. Or, he could have been right. He could have actually been the real deal.

The resurrection is Jesus' answer to back up all his statements about himself. Jesus didn't just have the courage to face death

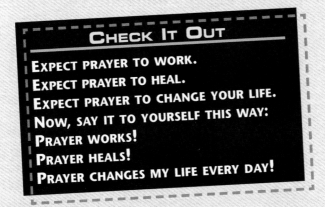

on the cross, he had the power to defeat it three days later. The resurrection is the event that shows that he was not an egomaniac or a madman. He was who he said he was: God's Son. Because of that he had power to defeat death and to truly bring us life. The resurrection is the exclamation point to Jesus' extraordinary life!

## CHECK IT OUT

EXPECT PRAYER TO WORK.
EXPECT PRAYER TO HEAL.
EXPECT PRAYER TO CHANGE YOUR LIFE.
NOW, SAY IT TO YOURSELF THIS WAY:
PRAYER WORKS!
PRAYER HEALS!
PRAYER CHANGES MY LIFE EVERY DAY!

Hey Steve,

One of my teachers at school said that the story of Jesus' resurrection is a nice story, but it's just that, a story. Is he right? Is there any historical reason to think the resurrection could really be a historical fact?

Fact or Fiction

Dear F or F,

Let me take a second to draw a distinction here that might be helpful to you. There are verifiable facts. There are probable or reasonable facts. There are fantasies. A verifiable fact is, "I sat in this chair yesterday, and it held me." A reasonable fact is, "Because that chair held me yesterday, I think it will hold me today." A fantasy is, "I'm going to sit in this chair and fly to the moon." The resurrection can never be a verifiable fact, but can it be reasonable fact or is it just a fantasy?

There are several interesting, easy-to-read books that are written by historians who have studied the resurrection. You could go to a big book store or look on the Internet for titles such as *Who Moved the Stone?* and *More Than a Carpenter*. These books won't give you 100 percent certainty; belief in any event 2,000 years ago takes an element of faith. They can help you feel confident that there are good, sound, intelligent reasons to believe that Jesus' resurrection was a lot more credible than believing in the Easter Bunny.

★ ◎ ★

## *WHY DO YOU BELIEVE?*

Why do you believe in the resurrection? If you came across this in a novel or a movie, you'd say, "No way! That never happened!" Believing in Jesus means believing in the resurrection. Think about your faith. List five reasons why *you* believe.

1.
2.
3.
4.
5.

★ ◎ ★

## *PURPOSEFUL PRAYER*

> **I am the resurrection and the life. Those who believe in me, even though they die, will live, and everyone who lives and believes in me will never die.**
> **JOHN 11:25-26**

**Dear God,**
So many things in the world around me are less than they promise to be. I thank you so much that I can trust you. Thank you that Jesus didn't just make big claims, but he actually lived them out. Help me trust that he can give me life, peace, forgiveness, and hope. I love you, God.
**Amen**

# DISCIPLESHIP MEANS...

> " Show me the path where I should walk, O Lord; point out the right road for me to follow. Lead me by your truth and teach me, for you are the God who saves me. All day long I put my hope in you. "
>
> **PSALM 25:4-5 NLT**

We all follow someone. Even if we are deeply committed to not conforming, we learn how to do that from nonconformists who came before us. The questions are who are you going to follow and will they lead you to a life that matters, a life of purpose? What does following a man who lived 2,000 years ago and never drove a car or watched a movie or used the Internet look like? These essays explore that question.

# To Have and to Hold, for Richer, for Poorer

> **66** I have been crucified with Christ; and it is no longer I who live, but it is Christ who lives in me. And the life I now live in the flesh I live by faith in the Son of God, who loved me and gave himself for me. **99**
> **GALATIANS 2:19-20**

Who are the people you have relationships with? Your friends. Your parents. Your teachers, coaches, band director, etc. If you have a job, you have relationships with your boss, fellow employees, and maybe customers. Perhaps you have a special someone you are going out with (or would like to be!); that is a relationship of an entirely different kind. You probably have a relationship with a great-aunt or two who still thinks you are five years old and gives you baby Christmas gifts. Some of these relationships might be pretty intense while others are casual. You might have incredibly positive feelings about some of your relationships and less positive feelings about others.

Throughout history, Christians have thought about the Christian life in terms of relationships. When a person decides to become part of the Christian faith, that person is not committing to an idea or a program. She or he is entering into a relationship. A relationship with God. So, what does that relationship look like? There are three images that have been the main images over the years. Let's look at them briefly with the main focus being upon the last. These images are the relationship of a king and his subjects, the relationship of a parent and a child, and the relationship of a husband and wife.

## King and Subjects

It's important to note what kind of king we're talking about here. If you read the Old Testament, you'll find God trying again and again to get the kings of Israel (God's people) to rule with mercy, justice for those in need, and an attitude of service. God isn't a king who demands slave labor or blind obedience. He's a king who rules with kindness and loving concern for his subjects. God made us. Everything we have is a gift, even ourselves. Not only did God create us and give us life as a gift, but God's Son, Jesus, died for our sins. That's why the Bible uses language like "you are not your own. You were bought with a price."

## Parent and Child

One of the most commonly known passages in the Bible is the Lord's Prayer. You might even know it by heart without realizing it. How does it start? "Our Father..." There are also verses throughout the Bible that use images of God being like a mother comforting a child. What kind of parent is God? Is he an absentee dad; is God a super-strict mom? In the New

Testament, we are encouraged to use the term *abba* when referring to our spiritual Father. That's an important word because it means "daddy," an emotionally close, caring, available parent.

## Husband and Wife

Perhaps the most significant relationship the Bible talks about is the relationship of marriage. When a marriage looks like God planned it to be, it's an amazing thing! It's not one member dominating the other. It's not drawing up a prenuptial agreement for who gets the antique dresser when things go bad. Marriage the way God intends it, and the image the Bible has in mind, is about two people mutually giving themselves to each other. There's not one member doing all the giving and the other all the taking or one member having all the power and the other having nothing.

In God's kind of marriage, both members are almost falling over one another to serve and to give to the other. Yes, the wife belongs to the husband, but only in the same way that the husband belongs to the wife. In God's marriage the TV would be tuned to the Lifetime channel just as often as to ESPN—and both spouses would like it!

*BUMPER STICKER THEOLOGY*

**THE CROSS: GOD'S ANSWER TO "DO YOU LOVE ME?"**

When you enter the Christian faith, you belong to God. Not as a slave to a master, but as two people who enter into a marriage and give themselves to each other. God wants you to give yourself to him, but he's already given all of himself to you!

## I Do. Do You?

Have you been to any weddings lately? Seen any on TV? Imagined one with someone special? List five things that are done or said that reflect the idea of two people giving themselves to one another:

1.
2.
3.
4.
5.

Now go back through the list and think about how these things relate to your relationship with God!

## I Need a Little Help Here!

Did you ever hear this famous quote from President John F. Kennedy? "Ask not what your country can do for you—ask what you can do for your country."

Well, how many times do you ask God to do something for you? Are your prayers always about you and what you need from God? Try this next time you pray. (How about right now?)

**Dear God,**

I just want you to know that I am here, and I am open to doing whatever I can to help you. I'm thankful for the strong presence you have in my life and everything you do for me—and I want to help you for a change! Please guide me toward the path where I can help you.
**Amen**

Try saying this prayer every day for a week. Keep a journal and record all the instances where you find yourself in a position to do God's good work. You just might be surprised!

## PRAYING FOR PURPOSE

> **You do not belong to yourself, for God bought you with a high price.**
> 1 CORINTHIANS 6:19-20 NLT

**Dear Lord,**

This week, I will work on building a strong relationship with you. I need to work on giving you as much as you give me. I know I'll never reach that goal, but help me keep trying to love you, trust you, rely on you, worship you as much as I possibly can—and not just on Sundays. I need to work on our relationship every day, all day long.

Thank you, Lord, for giving me your all, even when I fall short of giving you all of me!
**Amen**

# Talking to Others About God

> **"Publish his glorious deeds among the nations. Tell everyone about the amazing things he does."**
> **PSALM 96:3 NLT**

Sharing your faith in Jesus can be scary. Maybe you break out in a cold sweat just thinking about it. What will you say? What will people think of you? What if they laugh at you? We all know that God wants us to share Jesus with others. But that doesn't make doing it any easier, does it? Well, sit back and relax. No guilt trips here, okay? Let's take a look at why sharing our faith with others is so important. Then we'll share some tips that could help you start sharing Jesus today—and in ways that won't seem scary or strange.

The Bible tells us that the "harvest is plentiful" (Matthew 9:37). That means the world is full of people who are ready to receive the love and forgiveness of Jesus—but most of them don't even know it. You probably know some of them: your best friend; the guy in algebra class who irritates the snot out of you; or it could be your mom, dad, sister, or brother. But you can bet God sees each and every one of them, and he wants them to know how much better their lives can be—inside and out—if they accept Jesus.

The Bible also tells us that even though the harvest is so great, "the laborers are so few"

(Matthew 9:37). That means that even though there are people all around us who are ready to receive Christ, there are very few of us willing to give them that opportunity! We're either too busy or too scared to reach out to them. And that breaks Jesus' heart—I believe—for a couple of reasons.

**PONDER MORE!**

REMEMBER THAT IT'S NOT UP TO YOU TO CONVINCE ANYONE THAT JESUS IS THE WAY. THAT'S GOD'S JOB! ALL YOU HAVE TO DO IS SHARE YOUR FAITH WITH WORDS AND ACTIONS; GOD WILL DO THE REST.

The most obvious reason is that God wants those people to be saved, and no one takes the time to notice them or love them. They aren't getting the message that God cares simply because God's people refuse to care. But the other reason is that God wants to give each one of us the gift of sharing Jesus with others. It's not just for the other person, you know. It's also meant to be a gift to you—it's an amazing, adventurous experience telling others the most important message they'll ever hear.

Think about it: You get to play a part in God's eternal plan and feel the joy of knowing that God used you to love someone! Do you know what it feels like to share Jesus with someone and lead them to salvation? It's amazing! God wants to work through you to reach someone else with

**BUMPER STICKER THEOLOGY**

**TALK MAY BE CHEAP, BUT TALK ABOUT JESUS IS PRICELESS!**

his love. He wants you to grow closer to him through that experience.

But even with how cool and life-changing it can be, I know sharing your faith isn't necessarily easy. God understands your fears. And you can start out small. You don't have to go knocking on doors or talking to total strangers your first time out!

A great and simple way to get started is to make a list of five people in your life who need Jesus. Keep that list in a special place. Pray for those people daily. Ask God to get their hearts ready to receive Jesus. Ask God to use you in any way that he sees fit. Because the truth is that you may not be the person to lead them in a salvation prayer—but that's totally okay! It's just as important to be a link in that process. God might lead you to do special favors for them. Or he may lead you to ask them to youth group. There are many, many ways you can show them the love of Jesus—many ways for God to use you.

The important thing is to be open and available to God. And before you know it, you'll grow in your relationship with God and experience the joy of having him work through you!

## PURPOSEFUL PONDERABLE

Christians should behave differently than the rest of the world. When they do, people often want to know why. In 1 Peter 3:15–16, Peter says that you should be ready to answer questions about your faith—but you should be careful how you do it. Be gentle and respectful—don't beat others over their heads with your Bible! People may not always respond positively to what you have to say, but that's okay—it may be years later that they remember a conversation with you and respond. You never know! Just remember to speak with gentleness and respect—and you'll never feel badly if they didn't like what you had to say.

## PRAYING FOR PURPOSE

**Dear God,**
I want you to use me to bring people closer to you. I want you to use me to show your love. I admit that sometimes I get freaked out about sharing my faith with others. Sometimes I don't know what to say, or I'm afraid of what they'll think of me. Forgive me for the times when I've bailed because I was afraid. But thank you that you keep giving me chances to share my faith. I want to know the joy that comes from sharing Jesus with others. Help me see the opportunities you give me. Give me the courage to step out in faith and watch you work through me. God, please prepare the hearts of the people around me to hear about you. Give me the words to say when the time is right. In Jesus' name,
**Amen**

# Separating Myself from the World

“ **Cease to do evil, learn to do good; seek justice, rescue the oppressed, defend the orphan, plead for the widow.** ”
**ISAIAH 1:16-17**

"Discipleship means separating myself from the world." Hmmm…Sounds good. But what, exactly, does it mean to separate yourself from the world? It's a tricky concept, and it's important to understand.

First off, separating yourself doesn't mean isolating yourself. It is hard to touch others' lives if you are isolated from everyone. And we don't just mean physical isolation, such as living on top of a mountain all by yourself. Some people isolate themselves through their actions—by being extremely shy or by acting like they are more important than other people. If you feel

**BIBLE BITS & BYTES**

One of only two Bible books that never has the word "God" in it is the Book of Esther (the other is the Song of Songs). But Jewish rabbis did find God's holy name (Y-H-W-H, which stands for Yahweh) hidden in the first letter of four words found in an important part of the story. The rabbis believe that God is unseen but present in the book.

self-important because you are trying to live a worthy life, you've missed the point. Being separate in this way definitely isn't the correct path toward discipleship.

There *are* things of this world, however, that it's good to separate from. And doing so helps you get closer to Christ and closer to the worthy life you're striving for. Gossip,

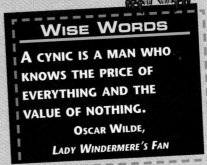

materialism, addiction to video games, these are examples of worldly things from which you should isolate yourself. Anything that pulls you from trying to live a worthy life is something to get rid of.

And you know what's really cool about all this? The more negative things you leave behind, the more Christ's love and direction can enter your life. When you make room for him, he fills the emptiness that's left when you give up something you don't need anymore. You become closer to God and better able to follow the path you've been called to.

The next step is *connecting* with the world in a new and better way. First off, you're connecting with Jesus as the center of your life as you strive for more knowledge and discipline. Notice that the focus of your connections will shift from *things* to

**BUMPER STICKER THEOLOGY**

**DISCIPLESHIP IS MY ANTI-DRUG!**

> **THE TRUE VALUE OF ANYTHING IS DETERMINED BY THIS AND THIS ALONE: DOES IT MAKE THE WORLD BETTER, HAPPIER, OR A MORE BEAUTIFUL PLACE?**

*people.* You'll connect with people in need—providing service in ways you may not even imagine right now. The Lord will help you find those who need you, whether it's by serving a meal at a shelter or mentoring a young boy who has no father. You will be connected to people in wonderfully loving ways.

So it all sounds pretty great, but you're wondering, "How do I do it? Who do I talk to? Where do I go?" Listen to your heart and soul. Does it call you to a life of discipleship? Do you have a sense of "mission"—a sense that you *have* to serve the Lord? Then all you have to do is make up your mind! Talk to your pastor, talk to your parents, and don't forget to talk to the Lord. Start praying and praying and praying. He'll be listening, and he will answer and show you the way.

**IS DISCIPLESHIP YOUR THING?**

IF IT IS, YOU'LL STRIVE FOR
- KNOWLEDGE
- DISCIPLINE
- GOOD HABITS/VIRTUE
- AWARENESS OF NEED
- THE WILLINGNESS TO SERVE THOSE IN NEED
- SETTING AN EXAMPLE OF A WORTHY LIFE

# PRAYING FOR PURPOSE

> *Do not be conformed to this world, but be transformed by the renewing of your minds, so that you may discern what is the will of God—what is good and acceptable and perfect.*
>
> **ROMANS 12:2**

**Dear Jesus,**

I want so much to follow your path of discipleship. Deep within my soul, I feel the need and the desire that calls me to this life with you. I know I'm still young, but I believe this to be my mission. I wish with my whole heart to put you at the center of my life. I want to become active in spreading belief and faith in you. I am working to live a life that is strong and filled with goodness so that I make you proud. I want to set an example with my actions as well as my words.

I try to see need around me, Lord Jesus, and to help out whenever I can. I pray that you will guide me to the ones who need my help—and I pray that I can see their need and that you will guide me in what to do.

Help me separate myself from the material things of this world that distract me from the path you have chosen for me. Already I can feel that this separation is bringing me closer to you and to my family in new and profound ways.

Thank you, Lord, for this calling and for showing me your love.

**Amen**

# Worshiping God
# Every Day

" I appeal to you therefore, brothers and sisters, by the mercies
of God, to present your bodies
as a living sacrifice, holy and
acceptable to God, which is
your spiritual worship. "
**ROMANS 12:1**

Quick—when you hear the word *worship,* what comes to mind? Sunday morning church service, praise songs, hymns? That's what most people think of when they hear the word *worship.* But I looked it up in the dictionary. Did you know that the definition never mentions music or singing? Instead, the dictionary defines worship as showing love and honor to God.

We certainly can show God that we love and honor him through the songs we sing at church on Sunday. But what about the rest of our lives? Worship should be more than just something we do for an hour once a week at church.

Imagine you're in church, and you see a man who looks lost in worship. His eyes are

---

**MAKE WORSHIP MORE THAN JUST A SONG YOU SING—MAKE IT A LIFE YOU LIVE IN JESUS' NAME.**

---

closed, you think you even see a tear trickle down his cheek—but he's smiling, too. Every once in a while he raises his hands. *Wow,* you think. *This guy must really love Jesus. How cool is that!*

You follow him out of the service. On the steps outside the church, a child runs across his path. The man starts screaming and cursing at the child.

Your mind would be reeling right? During the worship service, this guy certainly looked like he was showing love and honor to God. He seemed so sincere! Yet as soon as he walked out of the church, his behavior proved otherwise. You conclude that his worship wasn't truly worship. After all, nobody who really loves and honors God treats a child that way.

Drastic example—I know. But it illustrates what a lot of Christians do. We have no problem worshiping God on Sunday—when we think worship means singing songs about God and feeling good as we remember how much Jesus loves us. But something happens to us when we walk out the door and enter our week. We forget that worship means showing God that we love and honor him every single day of our lives! And we go about our activities not thinking much about God and what he would want us to do each day. Instead we get angry and yell at our parents, talk about others behind their backs, and worry about things that God wants us to give over to him.

## SOLO TIME

ONE OF THE BEST WAYS TO BUILD A LIFE OF WORSHIP IS TO SPEND TIME ALONE WITH GOD. SO TAKE TIME THIS WEEK TO WALK AND TALK WITH JESUS.

Worship is much more than what we do on Sundays at church. Worship is a lifestyle. In our Bible verse for this week, Paul wants the Christians in Rome to know that worship is about how you live your life. He wants them to know that the best way to show God we love and honor him is to give him our whole beings—our minds, our hearts, our spirits, and our actions. Our entire lives can be one big worship service to God!

So how are you doing these days worshiping God? If you're like most of us, you struggle with true worship. It's much easier to just go to church, sing some great songs, pray a little, hear an inspiring message, and go home. But that's not the kind of worship God *really* cares about.

Sure he loves it when we praise him on Sunday morning. He loves it when we gather together with other believers to support and pray for one another. He loves to hear our songs of love that we sing to him. But if we walk out of that service unchanged—if we think that worship is only about what we do at a church service, God is not impressed.

So the next time you leave a church service, take your heart of worship with you. Ask God to show you how you can worship him with your whole life in the days ahead. Make worship more than just a song you sing— make it a life you live in Jesus' name.

# FIVE IDEAS FOR BRINGING WORSHIP TO YOUR LIFE

1. Begin your day with prayer, and dedicate your day to God.
2. When you're around people who are gossiping, refuse to join in the conversation.
3. Be kind to someone who drives you crazy.
4. Give your mom, dad, grandma, uncle—whoever takes care of you—a hug and tell that person you love them.
5. Pray at least once during your day at school to remind yourself that God is with you.

## PRAYER WALK

Go for a walk with Jesus. (There's no goal or agenda to this prayer other than spending some time with your friend Jesus. Let him guide your time together.)

- Imagine that Jesus is actually walking right beside you.
- Walk in silence for a few minutes. Know that Jesus likes being with you.
- Give Jesus the concerns of your day, and tell him you don't want anything to come between the two of you as you walk and talk together. Tell him that you trust him to take care of all your concerns.
- Tell him you're open to anything he wants to say to you today.

• Just listen. Enjoy your surroundings. Notice sounds, smells, sights. Thank God for each one. But continue to listen for the voice of Jesus.

• Respond to what you think he's saying to you.

• When you sense God is done speaking, close your time with a prayer of thanks to God for always being with you.

• Make sure you find another Christian to talk to about your experience.

(NOTE: DON'T WORRY IF YOU DON'T "HEAR" ANYTHING. JUST WALKING WITH JESUS IN SILENCE CAN BE A VERY SATISFYING THING TO DO! SOMETIMES NO WORDS ARE NECESSARY BETWEEN GOOD FRIENDS.)

## *PRAYING FOR PURPOSE*

> **Make a joyful noise to the Lord, all the earth. Worship the Lord with gladness.**
> **PSALM 100:1-2**

**Dear God,**

Thanks for showing me what real worship is. It's great to know that worship isn't just about what we do on Sunday morning. And I really do want to worship you with my life. Forgive me for the times when I haven't taken worship seriously. Give me opportunities every day to show you that I love and honor you. When I fail to worship you with my life, remind me to ask you for forgiveness so I can start fresh. I do love you, God. Please show me how to make true worship something I do every single day. In Jesus' name I pray,
**Amen**

# You Gotta Step Out over the Edge

> " After this, Jesus went out and saw a tax collector by the name of Levi sitting at his tax booth. 'Follow me,' Jesus said to him, and Levi got up, left everything and followed him. "
> LUKE 5:27-28 NIV

It's summer and you're on that camping trip you've looked forward to all spring. Today it's not hiking through bug-infested woods, it's time for some real adventure. You're going rock climbing and rappelling. The group is seated at the top of the cliff while the guide explains how things work. She talks about belaying techniques, knots, carabiners, and rope strength. At the end of all of that she asks, "How many of you believe this rope will hold you as you go down the cliff?" Every hand goes up, including yours. Why not? You've heard the speech, seen the rope, seen the tree at the top to which the rope is anchored. No reason to doubt that rope will hold you.

PEOPLE FOLLOW ALL KINDS OF THINGS. THEY BECOME FANS OF THE LATEST DIET CRAZE, THE HOTTEST NEW BAND, THEIR FAVORITE SPORTS TEAM, OR THIS SUMMER'S COOLEST ACTOR. WHO BETTER TO "FOLLOW" THAN THE ONE PERSON WHOSE LIFE HAS MOST IMPACTED THE WORLD? FOLLOW JESUS!

"Great!" she says. "Now who's going over first?" Well, that changes everything. What was a raised hand a minute ago while you daydreamed about what would be in today's lunch is now much more serious business. All of a sudden your mouth is dry, and your pulse is racing. "Why don't you give it a try?" the guide says. There must be some mistake here—she's holding out the rope to you!

You get hooked in, trying desperately to pretend to your friends that you are really excited about this. "Hey, my hands always tremble and my face goes white as a sheet when I'm having fun!" You carefully inch your way over to the edge, where the guide says, "Now, the way this works is you have to just sit back and let all your weight go over the edge until the rope and harness catch you."

*Right! Let the rope catch me?! There's no way this flimsy rope is going to catch me! I'm going to tumble into oblivion,* your mind

**STEPPING OUT OVER THE EDGE TAKES FAITH!**

F OLLOW THE LORD.
A CKNOWLEDGE THAT THE PATH WILL NOT ALWAYS BE EASY.
I NVENT YOUR TRUST ANEW IF IT WAVERS.
T HANK GOD FOR TRUSTING YOU TO TACKLE SOMETHING NEW.
H AVE FAITH IN THE VOICE WITHIN.

screams. That's the whole point. It's one thing to believe in the safety of the rope and the knowledge of your guide when you're sitting safely on the ground. It's an entirely different thing to believe that as you step backward, leaning all your weight over the

Hey Steve,

At my church, they have been saying that Jesus wants people to not just believe him but follow him, too. Jesus lived so long ago and on the other side of the world. What does it look like to follow him 2,000 years later?

Just Getting Started

Dear JGS,

There are a few things that might help answer your question. One great way to find out how to follow Jesus is to look closely at his life. Reading the Gospels is a way to see how Jesus treated people and what he cared about. As you read, you'll get a sense of his priorities for your life.

A second way is to read other parts of the Bible that show you how Jesus' friends followed him. Read the Book of Acts and the letters Paul, Peter, and others wrote in the New Testament to give you practical advice and examples on what following Jesus looks like.

Finally, I'd recommend finding some people in your community who have been followers of Christ for longer than you. Talk to them, get to know them. Maybe there are some older students in your youth group, a youth group leader, an adult in your church, or a pastor or priest who you respect and could learn from. Good luck!

edge, to discover if it's all really trustworthy.

Surveys say the vast majority of Americans believe in God and his Son, Jesus. For many people, it's a kind of sitting-safe-on-the-ground-on-top-of the-cliff belief. When Jesus met people during his life, he never asked them, "Hey, do you think I'm a good guy? Do you think I'm a wise teacher?" He said to them, "Follow me."

The kind of belief Jesus is interested in is not an absent-minded, abstract kind of deal, it is a stake-your-life-on-it, lean-back-over-the-cliff, and if-this-rope-doesn't-hold-I'm-in-big-trouble kind of faith. Jesus is interested in people who are really going to follow him; he wants more from us than a checkmark on some survey saying we agree that he exists.

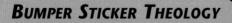

### BUMPER STICKER THEOLOGY

## NEED DIRECTION? FOLLOW JESUS.

You see, Jesus believed that he was coming to make a difference for all of humanity. He said, "I am the light of the world." His was a life that mattered, and he's interested in people who want to live a life filled with that kind of meaning and purpose, too. A purposeful life isn't lived from the sidelines, you've got to get in the game. You've got to take the plunge!

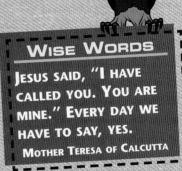

**WISE WORDS**

JESUS SAID, "I HAVE CALLED YOU. YOU ARE MINE." EVERY DAY WE HAVE TO SAY, YES.
MOTHER TERESA OF CALCUTTA

## PRAYING FOR PURPOSE

> **Keep alert, stand firm in your faith, be courageous, be strong. Let all that you do be done in love.**
> 1 CORINTHIANS 16:13–14

**Dear God,**
I want to take the plunge and follow you, but sometimes I'm scared. What will my friends say? What will my family say? Will I make a fool of myself? Well, I guess I just need to trust that you'll show me how to best take this life-changing plunge into following you. Give me the courage, the strength, and the ability I need to become your disciple. Help me not worry about what people may say. Let me follow you and bring glory to your name!
**Amen**

# Loving Even My Enemies

> **Bear with one another and, if anyone has a complaint against another, forgive each other; just as the Lord has forgiven you, so you also must forgive.**
> **Colossians 3:13**

Buzz had tormented Lilly on a daily basis (every school day, anyway) since they were six years old. That's when Buzz's family moved to town and joined Lilly's first-grade class. There were one or two blissful years in their small elementary school when they were in different classes, but otherwise they were right there together. Buzz's last name was Miffler. Lilly's? Middleton. That meant that when kids were seated on the first day of school, there was Buzz, right behind Lilly in alphabetical order.

Middle school was better; Lilly only had four classes with Buzz during the three years. And high school was a dream come true with just the occasional remark in passing as Buzz happened to walk by her in the hall.

Lilly never knew why he did it. But he

**BIBLE BITS & BYTES**
God is love, and those who abide in love abide in God, and God abides in them.
1 John 4:16

continued tormenting her through the years. It started with her red hair and freckles, and it didn't help that she was always the tallest girl. Each day he'd come to school having carefully prepared his homework from the night before. And his homework seemed to focus on coming up with yet another horrible name to call Lilly. The number of names he had called her over the years was astonishing.

Lilly's family was quite religious, and Jesus had been at the heart of their family life ever since she could remember. Prayer, faith, and worship just came naturally for Lilly. She loved it; she loved Christ! As she got into high school and learned about discipleship, she felt it was a natural path for her. In fact, it wasn't anything different from how she had lived her entire life. Except for one thing. She knew that she was supposed to love *everyone,* even her enemies.

At first when she had studied this idea with her pastor, she chuckled at the thought that she had, or would ever have, an enemy. Lilly was a quiet young woman, an honors student; she participated in student council, was on the yearbook staff, and was a star basketball player. (Being 5'11" had finally paid off!) She loved school and all her activities and never faltered in her faith and her ultimate focus on the Lord.

## WANT TO TRULY LIVE? FORGIVE!

Then one day she was walking down the hall at school and there he was—Buzz. He smiled and waved! *Yes!* thought Lilly. *He's changed!* They passed each other, and he was still smiling. But there was something in his smile that wasn't sincere. "Loser!" he called as he knocked her books to the floor. By the time she looked up, he was gone. *I hate him!* she thought.

The next time her pastor discussed loving enemies, Lilly was really upset. How could she *love* Buzz? She knew she had to love him, but it just seemed an impossible task. Lilly struggled with the Buzz situation for several months. She talked about it a lot with Jesus, with her pastor, and with her parents. They all helped her see that holding negative feelings for someone was really only hurting her. It was taking energy she needed and wanted to use for good. It was interfering with her goal of keeping Jesus and his ways at the core of her life each and every day. When she finally let go of the negativity, she felt lighter somehow, like when your shoulders are all hunched up with tension and then someone comes along and gives you a massage and you just go "ahhhhhhhhh." Suddenly everything was better.

Did Buzz pick up on her attitude change and become her friend? It would be great if after a few weeks of Lilly's new attitude, Buzz softened and the insults stopped. But that didn't happen. Sometimes it does, though. We can't control what another person thinks, feels, or does. We can only control ourselves, and that's what counts.

Do you have any enemies? Are you ready to let go and love them?

## FORGIVENESS

Is there someone you consider your enemy? Write that person's name here:

_____

Now visualize that person. Put them in a chair or maybe up on a small stage. Imagine you're talking to them, "I want you to know that I forgive you for anything you've ever done that was harsh or cruel or unfriendly. I believe you are a good person at heart and that you are always doing the very best you can do at the moment. I pray that some day we will no longer have any differences. Please accept this forgiveness and know that I have no bad feelings toward you. I let go of my anger and hatred. I forgive you."

Now put yourself in that chair or on the stage. Speak to yourself: "I want you to know that I forgive you for feeling anger or hatred toward

_____

There were many reasons for you to feel that way, and it is understandable. I know you will let go of those bad feelings and move into God's light where there is only room for love in your heart. I love you, and I forgive you."

## BUMPER STICKER THEOLOGY

## LOVE: IT DOES A SOUL GOOD!

## PRAYING FOR PURPOSE

> " Then Peter came and said to him, 'Lord, if another member of the church sins against me, how often should I forgive? As many as seven times?' Jesus said to him, 'Not seven times, but, I tell you, seventy-seven times.' "
> **MATTHEW 18:21-22**

**Father,**

I know that Jesus turned the other cheek and held no grudge against anyone. I am trying my best to be like that, but it isn't easy. Please stand with me and help me learn how to do this. I want only to live a life that is right and true to everything you stand for. It's just that this stuff about loving my enemies isn't always so easy to do, no matter how badly I want to do it.

I know you are always with me and my faith will keep me going and working on this. Thank you, Lord, for always being there and showing me the way. I'm thankful for your help!

**Amen**

# Developing the Discipline of Prayer

> **One day Jesus was praying in a certain place. When he finished, one of his disciples said to him, 'Lord, teach us to pray.'**
> **LUKE 11:1 NIV**

Jesus prayed and taught his 12 disciples to pray. Since we're Jesus' disciples, too, that means prayer is important in our lives. We all know we should probably pray more than we do, but maybe you aren't sure how to pray or wonder if you're doing it right. Maybe praying bores you. Or maybe you just have a hard time figuring out what to say to God.

You're not alone! Lots of people struggle with their prayer lives. But it doesn't have to be that way. Prayer can be one of the coolest things you get to do in your walk with Jesus. And I'm excited to share with you some ways you can develop a life of prayer.

The first thing to remember is that we can pray to God for all different kinds of reasons. We can pray when we have concerns. We can ask God to help us through a time of trouble. We can pray when we need him to forgive us for something wrong we said or did. We can pray when we're lonely and need to remember that he loves us. We can pray when we're happy and want to thank God for all the good things he's done for us. We can pray when we want to tell God how great he is. We can pray to tell God we love him. We can pray to simply say "hello" to God!

There's no limit to the reasons for prayer. And we can pray anywhere we want. In bed, in the shower, on a walk, at school, even while driving. (Just make sure you don't close your eyes behind the wheel!)

The second thing to remember is that prayer is a conversation between you and God. You have conversations with your friends all the time. Sometimes you talk, other times you listen to what they have to say. It's the same deal with prayer.

People often think prayer is only about asking God to do a bunch of stuff. (No wonder we get bored if all we're doing in prayer is reading our "to do" list to God.) But that's not how God sees prayer at all.

Sure God loves it when we go to him with all our concerns and ask him for things, which shows we believe he has the power to meet our needs. But God also loves it when we give him the chance to talk to us. And God will talk to us in all sorts of ways when we pray.

God may give you a sense of peace after you tell him about a struggle you're having. Or he may lead you to a Bible verse to help you in your situation. He could also lead you to speak to someone. Or he may draw you to worship him as the God who has perfect control over your life. He might not give you an answer to your concerns, but you may realize you don't need an answer right now—your trust in God is enough to get through whatever is troubling you.

Finally, we need to remember to make time in our lives for prayer, because prayer is the number one way we get close to God. The Bible teaches us lots of things *about* God, but it's in prayer that we really get to *know* God. If you read a stranger's journal, you'll learn lots of stuff about that person's life, but you wouldn't really *know* that stranger. Now think about all the time you've spent with your friends talking about things that are important to you—those friends are the people who know you best. It's the same way with God and prayer.

God wants you to know him and experience the joy of prayer. Let these next seven days be the beginning of a new commitment to spending more time with God in prayer. You'll be glad you did.

## PRAYER EXPERIMENT #1:
## LECTIO DIVINA

*Lectio divina* is Latin for "divine reading." It's based on the belief that every time we read the Bible, God has something to say to us. When you pray in the style of *lectio divina*, you read a passage of Scripture slowly and let God speak to you through the words of the passage.

Set aside 15 minutes for this, but you can go longer if you want.

- Grab your Bible, and go to a quiet place where no one will disturb you.
- Pick out a story from one of the Gospels— Matthew, Mark, Luke, or John. Short passages that tell a story are best for this.
- Spend a few moments in silence to quiet yourself down.
- If any concerns or thoughts come to mind, give them to God.
- Briefly ask God to be with you in this time of prayer and to speak to you anyway he wants.
- When you feel ready, begin slowly reading the passage you chose.
- Read it at least three times—*slowly* each time.
- As you read, listen for a word or a phrase that jumps out at you.
- When something in the passage catches your attention, stop.
- Ask God what he might be trying to say to you in that word or phrase.

- Now just listen.
- Have a conversation with God about what he's telling you.
- In closing, write down what you think God said to you.

(Share your prayer experience with a trusted Christian friend.)

## PRAYER EXPERIMENT #2: THE JESUS PRAYER

To keep in touch with God all day, try this simple prayer:

- Every time the bell rings at school, say the name *Jesus* to yourself silently.
- As you say his name, let it remind you that Jesus is always with you every moment of the day and that he loves you. Notice how remembering Jesus throughout the day affects your thoughts, attitudes, and feelings.
- When you get home, write down what you experienced.
- Pray and thank Jesus for being with you all day.

### BIBLE BITS & BYTES

Obadiah is the shortest book in the Old Testament; it has only 21 verses. In the book, the prophet Obadiah blasts the Edomites, people who lived southeast of the Dead Sea, for rejoicing in the downfall of Jerusalem.

# PRAYER EXPERIMENT #3: ART PRAYER

Set aside at least 20 minutes for this. It's so fun, you'll probably end up spending more time!

- Gather some art supplies: paper, pens, crayons, colored pencils, clay, paint and brushes, glitter, and glue. Anything you have on hand will work.
- Keep your Bible on hand in case you need it. (God may lead you to a specific passage as you pray.)
- Spend a few moments in silence.
- Tell God about the day/week you just had.
- Thank him for the good things, and ask him for help with the bad things.
- Ask God to show you where he is at work in your life. (This is where your Bible may come in handy. If you don't get a verse, that's okay—just keep going with the prayer time.)
- Create a picture/drawing/anything that represents where and how God is at work in your life. (You don't have to show anyone this. It can be just between you and God.)
- Put your creation in your Bible or in some other special place so you can refer to it whenever you want to remember how God is at work in your life.
- Close your time by thanking God for giving you this experience.

# PRAYING FOR PURPOSE

**Dear God,**
I really want to spend more time with you in prayer. I'm so glad that you actually want to talk with me. When I really stop to think about it, it's amazing that you care about everything I tell you when I pray. And it's even more amazing that you want to share your thoughts and feelings with me! Help me to make time to pray more often. Help me to realize that prayer doesn't have to be a boring chore, but that it's something I can look forward to every day. And thanks, God, that you hear each prayer. In Jesus' name,
**Amen**

# You Can't Know Your Part Without Reading the Script!

> " My child, keep my words and store up my commandments with you; keep my commandments and live, keep my teachings as the apple of your eye; bind them on your fingers, write them on the tablet of your heart. "
> **PROVERBS 7:1-3**

If you've gone to church often or been a Christian for long, you might have had someone tell you that you should spend time reading the Bible. In fact, you should read it every day. Your first thought is probably that sitting in detention sounds more exciting. After all, the Bible is a 1,000-plus page book filled with rules and people and places that are so old and distant you can't even pronounce their names, right? "Come on, maybe if it came with a music video or something."

Well, here are a couple ways to think about the Bible that might help. First, what kind of things do you like to read? Have you ever received a love note? If you're a strapping high school guy, you'll never admit it publicly, but even the toughest of us melts a bit when a love note's in our hands. You pour over every word, "Dear Jim." (Wow, I'm dear to her, and she spelled my name right!) You read each sentence over and over, soaking it up and looking for

the secret meanings behind each phrase. Maybe it's even interactive: "Do you want to go out? Check one: yes___ no___ maybe___." You are in love, and it feels great to know that the other person loves you, too.

Think of the Bible that way. It is an extended love letter from God to you. Whether in stories that say, "See, look what I did for humanity, can't you see I'm crazy about you guys?" or poetry, or advice, the Bible is God saying again and again, "Hey world, I love you like mad!" Read the Bible like you read those love letters. Look for messages on each page, in each story, about how much God cares for you.

Second, and let's be honest, who hasn't read a book or sat in the dark of the movie theater and put themselves in the story? We all do it. We are the hero who saves the world, the daredevil who defies death to get the treasure, or the champion of the underdog sports team that upsets the heavy favorite. We love a great story, but even more, we love to dream that great stories might happen to us.

The Bible spans several hundred years and has a cast of characters that numbers in the thousands, but it really boils down to one story: God made the world and loves us. We wander away, get lost and in all kinds of trouble. God fights danger, death, and overwhelming odds to find us and bring us home. It starts in Genesis with the stories of the first people on earth and goes all the way to Revelation, where God's goodness finally and completely saves the day.

But, and here's the kicker, there's more to it than just a great story. This is one where we *are* actually invited to jump up on screen and take part in the action. In Hebrews 11, the author gives a summary of some of the great heroes of the Bible and what God did in their lives. Cool stuff. Then it gets better. At the start of chapter 12, the writer essentially says, "Hey, you've heard all these great stories, seen the first legs of this great relay race across time—now it's your turn! They're handing the baton to you."

As you read the Bible, you'll discover not

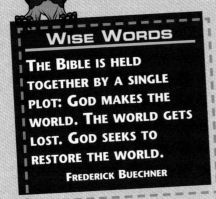

**WISE WORDS**

THE BIBLE IS HELD TOGETHER BY A SINGLE PLOT: GOD MAKES THE WORLD. THE WORLD GETS LOST. GOD SEEKS TO RESTORE THE WORLD.

FREDERICK BUECHNER

only a world of exciting stories of how God used men and women in history, but you'll discover your part in the great story. God is up to big things and wants you to be in on the action. How can you know your lines without reading the script?

## BEYOND THE BIBLE

The Bible is absolutely required reading on your journey toward discipleship. But guess what? There are tons of other wonderful books out there on religion that offer different perspectives and points of view to get you excited about and thinking about Christianity in new and different ways. Both fiction and non-fiction books have something to offer.

So start a book club! You can do this with a group of like-minded friends or your church youth group.

Start with one book; pick something that looks interesting to you and is easy for everyone to get a copy. Set up a meeting in three weeks. Have everyone come with a list of three things the book makes them want to talk about. Get together to

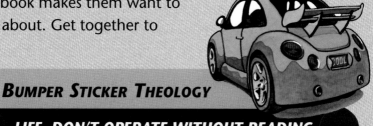

### BUMPER STICKER THEOLOGY

**LIFE. DON'T OPERATE WITHOUT READING THE OWNER'S MANUAL: THE BIBLE**

discuss what you've read. Be sure another member has chosen another book for the next meeting.

Don't forget to have everyone bring a snack to share!

**BIBLE BITS & BYTES**

Think you know the story of Jesus' birth really well? Well, what about those three wise men? Actually, the Bible never mentions that there are three men, only that there were three gifts given to the baby Jesus: gold, frankincense, and myrrh.

## PRAYING FOR PURPOSE

> " Now the parable is this: The seed is the word of God....But as for that in the good soil, these are the ones who, when they hear the word, hold it fast in an honest and good heart, and bear fruit with patient endurance. "
>
> LUKE 8:11, 15

**Dear God,**

I want to know you better. I want to know how you feel about me and how you want me to live my life. I believe the Bible can help me with all those things. As I read, help me understand what I read. Help me hear your voice in the words I read.

**Amen**

# Respecting My Parents

" **Children, obey your parents in everything, for this is your acceptable duty in the Lord.**
COLOSSIANS 3:20 "

Why do my parents constantly tell me what to do? Why do they snoop through my stuff? Why do they always want to know where I'm going? Why do they try to control my life?

Do your parents do any of this? Well, I hope they do! Now, you are thinking: *What? Are you nuts? This book is supposed to be for teens, not for parents! It's supposed to be supporting me, not them. I don't get it.*

Okay. The truth is that there is only one side to any of this, and that's the Lord's side! And we're all in the same spot on that, right? God gave us parents to love us, nurture us, and help us find him and keep him central in our lives. As Christians we know that it's up to us to love and respect everyone— all our fellow human beings and creatures. And we also know from the Bible that we're specifically commanded to

honor, cherish, and respect our parents. And that means even when they're driving us crazy. (Which may seem like most of the time!) Odds are they are only doing their job. God wants parents to raise their children in a loving and safe environment and to teach them respect and discipline. So when your mom and dad are making rules and checking up on you, it's because they are doing their job according to the job description God has laid out for them.

Now how does all this relate to discipleship? When you are following a path toward discipleship, you must truly understand and accept that disciple-ship means respecting your parents. Let's run that by again: To follow the path of discipleship, you must wholeheartedly respect your parents. This can be a tough thing to do during your teen years when every part of yourself is wanting to be out on your own. You may feel that you are indeed walking in the light of the Lord and are ready to be trusted with fewer rules. The truth is that working through this relationship with your parents is part of your path. It is one of the lessons you are learning. Standing on the path *with* your parents is what God intends. Only when you are

*Dear Jenny,*

*I'm trying to follow a path of discipleship and maintain faith and trust in the Lord. The problem is my parents. I'm supposed to respect them, but it's really hard. They're both alcoholics. How can I respect them? Why should I respect them? How can I follow God's commandment to honor them? If I don't obey the commandment, how can I lead a holy life?*
*Losing Sight of the Lord*

Dear Losing Sight,

You've got an incredibly difficult situation to live with. I really respect the fact that in the middle of all this you are finding the courage and the strength to walk with the Lord. Don't give up! The Lord will give you strength.

To answer your questions, we have to think hard about what God is telling us. He tells us to obey and respect our parents. In your situation, that may seem like a strange and impossible request.

You've already taken the first step in coping, and that is to choose the Lord over the path of your parents—it is that choice that will see you through. It may help you to try and look past your parents as people who make your life difficult. Can you try to look at them as people who are deeply troubled and ill? They have a disease. They also have a child they love very much, even if they don't show it. They are doing the best they can. Let me say that again: They are doing the best they can. It may not seem like it to you or to me, and we certainly wish they would change and do better. But you can't ever change another person. What you can change is how you respond to them. Respond to your parents with love and compassion. Ignore their drinking and anger, and try not to let it interfere with your walk with the Lord. Pray for God to help them become sober. Above all, respect that they are doing the very best they can in each and every moment. Pray about this, and ask your youth pastor for guidance as well. You are on a joyous journey with God, and this is one branch across the road. Be assured that God's love will be with you every step of the way.

**P** REPARING YOU FOR THE WORLD

**A** LWAYS THERE WHEN YOU NEED 'EM (AND EVEN WHEN YOU DON'T)

**R** ELY ON THEM

**E** VERYBODY'S GOT 'EM!

**N** OBODY CAN EVER REPLACE YOUR MOM AND DAD

**T** OTAL UNCONDITIONAL LOVE

**S** ING THEIR PRAISES!

old enough and understand well enough what it means to show respect, understanding, and love will you be directed to move on from this place.

So, what to do? When you get frustrated and feel yourself being anything less than totally respectful, seek answers. Pray to Jesus. Ask for patience and understanding. Talk to your pastor. Ask for ideas for staying on the path of virtue you have chosen. Talk with your friends. This is helpful in two different ways. First, if you talk to your peers, you'll see that you don't have the worst, the most unreasonable, or the nosiest parents. Second, you can help each other get through the tough times. Talk to your parents, even. Tell them that you are having trouble finding the feelings that you know are right.

They can help you understand why they do and say the things that they must.

God created families to be a loving and nurturing environment where we can mature. Make use of this wonderful gift by showing your parents all the love and respect they deserve!

## PRAYING FOR PURPOSE

" **Children, obey your parents in the Lord, for this is right. 'Honor your father and mother'—this is the first commandment with a promise: 'so that it may be well with you and you may live long on the earth.'** "
**EPHESIANS 6:1-3**

**Lord,**
Thank you for my parents. I am very thankful for them. I know they aren't perfect, but they are doing the best they can. Thank you for helping me keep this in mind on the days I forget and am disrespectful and rude. I love my parents, and I pray for the courage and strength to show them my love. I ask for your help in allowing me to bless them and make them proud as I live my life for you. Since I don't say it often, I'd like to thank you again for my parents.

Thank you for all the many blessings I enjoy.
**Amen**

# Where Did You Get That Accent?

Do you ever wonder how we become the people we are? Why do some of us talk with an accent that makes "park the car" sound like "paaak the caaaw"? Or why some of us say, "Yo, what's up" while others say, "howdy, ma'am"? After all, it's not like we are given a handbook when we are two that teaches people in Minnesota to say "yaa, you betcha." Infants aren't handed an interactive DVD on how to have a southern drawl.

If we live in one part of the country it's soda; if we live in another it's pop. If we live in a chemistry lab, it's a sugar-enriched carbonated beverage.

So where do all the particular ways we act and talk come from? Psychologists could probably give you all kinds of studies and theories, but really it's pretty simple. Bottom line is, we end up

speaking like, acting like, maybe even looking like the people we spend our time with. Your parents spent some time trying to teach you new words when you were little, but you ended up learning tons of stuff that they never taught you. You learned by being around people. The accent you have is the same as the accent of the people you grew up around. The slang you use is probably pretty similar to the slang the people around you use.

We learn by watching, listening, and just being with other people. We do more than just learn, though. We actually *become* like the people we spend time with when we were young or spend time with now. It happens without us even trying or thinking about it. Donald Trump's hit TV show is built around the same idea of finding a young apprentice who will follow and learn from him, so he or she can become a junior Donald Trump.

Living the kind of life God wants us to live is the same. Near the end of his life, Jesus said to his closest friends, people who had been with him day in and day out for three years, "I have

set you an example that you should do for others as I have done for you." In other words, you've watched me, now do what you have seen. And they did. Take Peter. He started out as a fisherman who got into trouble for speaking without thinking and getting into fights. After spending time with Jesus and following his example, Peter became a man who spoke to crowds about God's love, and he offered a healing hand to a crippled man (Acts 2–3). He became the kind of person who pleases God because he imitated Jesus' life.

That's what God has in mind for you. You did not live 2,000 years ago and walk around Jerusalem with Jesus, but you can look every day at who Jesus was and what he did. You can spend time every day reading the Gospels, the first four books of the New Testament, and learning how to live life by Jesus' example. If you are a guy, you can look at the dignity and respect that Jesus showed to women. At school you can show the care and concern to people that others have passed by or viewed as insignificant.

You learned how to talk just by hanging around grown-ups who talked. Learn how to live by hanging around Jesus, the Author of Life. Take time every day to read his story so that eventually it will become part of who you are, too.

## LIST IT!

List five things you did this week that are things Jesus would've done:

1.
2.
3.
4.
5.

List five things you did this week that he wouldn't have done:

1.
2.
3.
4.
5.

What will you do differently next week?

*Hey Steve,*

*It seems like most of my friends at school have gotten into drugs and drinking the last semester. What should I do? I don't want to go along, but I want to have friends. What would Jesus do in my situation?*
*Last One Sober*

Dear Last,

Jesus responded to temptation and his friends in various ways. While always remaining true to his convictions and making wise choices, he at times removed himself from a situation, and at other times he enthusiastically attended the fun parties.

So, what can you do? Here are three principles that could help.

1. When Jesus was really tired (and probably at his most vulnerable), he removed himself from the crowd and spent time in prayer and with friends he could trust. *In situations where you'll be vulnerable, lean on God and surround yourself with people who'll back you up.*

2. When Jesus was at a party, it was for a purpose. He was there out of concern for the others, and he wanted to show them a different and better way to live. Your friends need someone who will not join in with and approve of what they do but will still care for them. *There will be times when you can be that person, but remember principle one!*

3. Finally, Jesus spent most of his time with people who cared for one another, cared for him, and loved God. In the long run, if your friends only care about you if you mess yourself up making the same poor choices they do, you need new friends. *You need people who care about you and want what is best for you, not people who like you only if you follow the crowd.*

People who care about you are out there just waiting to meet you. It's not easy making new friends, but pray about it and ask for God's help. He will answer your prayers!

**Dear Jesus,**

I am trying my best to live a life according to your example, but it's not always easy. You were a pretty incredible guy! For today, I promise to think of you as I make each decision, even if it seems strange. Just for today, I'll do this and see what happens. If I take it day by day, I know I can lead a life that follows your example.

I pray that there might just be a little bit of you in me each and every day, and that I might pass that along to those who know me. Thank you so very much, Jesus. I love you and all you are.

**Amen**

## PRAYING FOR PURPOSE

> **Beloved, do not imitate what is evil but imitate what is good. Whoever does good is from God; whoever does evil has not seen God.**
> **3 JOHN 11**

**Dear God,**

I want to know how you want me to live my life. Help me to look to your Son, Jesus, as the example of what kind of life pleases you. Give me the courage to follow him through the halls of school today. Thank you, God, that Jesus showed me all I need to know about who you are and who I can be.

**Amen**

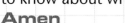

# LIFE'S CHALLENGES

> **Here on earth you will have many trials and sorrows. But take heart, because I have overcome the world.**
> JOHN 16:33 NLT

All of us reach times when we are out of answers. We reach moments where we don't know what to do or where to turn. God promises us two things: He is strong (able to help), and he is loving (motivated to help). That's a great combination. These essays are just some of the ways we can find support and solutions in life's challenging moments.

# Am I Being All I Can Be?

" **Lazy people want much but get little, while the diligent are prospering.** "
PROVERBS 13:4 LB

Are you perfect? Do you think you should be? Do you feel you're being all you can be? Are you living up to the potential the Lord has in mind for you? Are you approaching activities with the proper attitude, or are you so focused on being the best that you lose sight of life's purpose?

Wow. It might not seem so, but that's a lot of stuff to think about and discuss. You might say, "Hey, I'm a good student, I'm in band, I work on the school newspaper, I play soccer, I help out with the church youth group, and I volunteer at the humane society. This chapter doesn't apply to me." Guess again. It might even apply to you more than to those who are being a tad lazy and not getting much done!

Surprised? Life is all about surprises and challenging ourselves to live the very best we can. And

> **DON'T BE THE MOST YOU CAN BE, BE THE BEST YOU CAN BE!**

that doesn't mean doing the most stuff you can possibly pack into a day. The key is to listen to the Lord and live up to your potential. It's the "listening to the Lord" part that keeps us on track. Some people get so caught up in *doing* everything and always being the absolute *best* that they lose sight of what's truly important about living a good life. It's not about *how much* you do; it's about the choices you make about *what* you do and the quality of how you do it. Quality—not quantity—when it comes to activities. And it's not about being *the* best; it's about being *your* best!

Check this out: Mark was a good student. Not at the top of his class, but he usually got Bs. He was working hard and doing the best—*his* best. Some of his friends from church were straight-A students. He was usually okay with them talking about grades and stuff, but it slowly started to get to him. He wanted an A. He wanted to be *the* best. So he cheated on a test. He wrote out the difficult answers on a tiny slip of paper and cupped it in his hand. He was sure he'd get caught, but he didn't. And he got an A+. The highest grade

in the class. It felt really good. For about a day. Then he realized that not only had he sinned by cheating, but he had totally gotten off track of living the kind of life he was striving for. The A+ wasn't *his.* God's expectations for us are to live worthy lives, do good work, and be the absolute best person we can be. Mark had already been doing that!

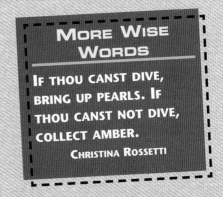

So when you get out your day planner and are organizing all your activities, keep in mind that the point is not to race around and do everything you can; the point is to do the things you tackle with your whole heart and with spirit. Always remember the true meaning and purpose of the things you do. Be your absolute best, and everyone will be proud—your parents, your Lord, and you!

## IS PRAYER A CRUTCH?

Janice got a C on her advanced algebra test. *That prayer sure didn't get answered!* she thought to herself as she folded the just-returned test paper and stuffed it deep into her backpack. Janice leads a worthy life; she works at keeping Christ central in all that she does. In fact, she had been so busy all week volunteering with her church youth group that she had neglected to study for the algebra test. So she had prayed exceptionally hard, asking God to help her out because she had been busy helping him out. Then, when she didn't get the grade she wanted, she blamed him for not answering her prayer.

Is this what prayer is all about? Can we expect to take it easy and then pray for what we want and expect it to be dropped in our lap? Of course not. You know that. Janice knows that. She just got caught up with being too busy to do her best and thought prayer would fix it.

Prayer isn't an easy way out. And we don't build up credit just because we're living a God-centered life. Remember the old saying: "God helps those who help themselves"? Well, that's what it's all about. If you want a good grade, study hard. And then pray!

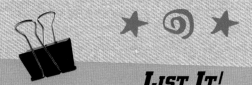

## List It!

List 1: List all the things you do, such as school, playing instruments, volunteering, etc.

1.
2.
3.
4.
5.
6.
7.

List 2: List the activities in order of importance to living your life according to God's plan.

1.

2.

3.

4.

5.

6.

7.

Is there anything you need to drop?

List 3: List anything you'd like to do to enhance your life that you're not yet doing. List them in order of importance.

1.

2.

3.

List 4: List the top four items from list 2 and add the top two items from list 3.

1.

2.

3.

4.

5.

6.

There! Now you have a list of six things (or less, that's okay) that you really want to do and will help you live a good, virtuous life according to Jesus' plan. Before you add anything more, be sure to evaluate why you want to do it and decide if you have time to truly give it your all.

## PRAYING FOR PURPOSE

> **So I tell you, whatever you ask for in prayer, believe that you have received it, and it will be yours.**
> **MARK 11:24**

**Lord,**

I wish to be all that I can be. I know you have laid out such a wonderful life for me—filled with opportunities and blessings. Yet, sometimes I guess I'm just lazy, and I don't reach for all the goals I know I can attain. Lord, I ask for your help and guidance in keeping me moving toward being all I can be and all you want me to be. I wish to live a life that I can be proud of and that you and my parents can be proud of, too!

**Amen**

# Does How I Dress Matter?

" **But the Lord said to Samuel, 'Do not look on his appearance or on the height of his stature, because I have rejected him; for the Lord does not see as mortals see; they look on the outward appearance, but the Lord looks on the heart.' "**
**1 SAMUEL 16:7**

There are two ways to look at this question. Let's discuss two perspectives that answer the question two ways.

First, you already know that how you dress makes a difference in many different situations. You probably dress differently to go see your Grandma than you do to go, say, to a rock concert. And you probably dress differently for church than you do for school. Dressing in a way that's appropriate to the situation and occasion is something we learn to do as part of being a responsible, social human being.

Beyond that, we base a lot of our impressions of people on how they dress. Whether that is good or bad, right or wrong, we all do it to a certain extent. Say Sara and Jane both go on a job interview to be a waitress at a neighborhood café that serves mostly

elderly people. Sara comes dressed in her usual torn jeans, nose ring, and tight fitting T-shirt. Jane dresses for the occasion in a knee-length skirt and blouse. Everything else being totally equal—demeanor, skills, experience—we can bet that Jane will get hired. Why? Because she knew that how she dressed mattered. It's not about discrimination; it's not about freedom of expression. It's about common sense and practicality.

Now let's look at the question in another way. Does God care how you dress? Michael always dresses every bit the rebellious teen: His hair color changes weekly to suit his mood, he wears more jewelry than his mom, and his clothes always look like he slept in them. Michael is also president of his church youth group, he works with the physically challenged after school, and he hangs out with kids who never drink, do drugs, or have sex. John always wears a neat

> **BIBLE BITS & BYTES**
>
> Don't be concerned about the outward beauty that depends on fancy hairstyles, expensive jewelry, or beautiful clothes. You should be known for the beauty that comes from within, the unfading beauty of a gentle and quiet spirit, which is so precious to God.
>
> 1 PETER 3:3–4 NLT

**God,**

I'm trying to be less focused on outward appearance and more focused on inner characteristics. I want to be comfortable enough with myself that I'm not always worrying about how I look. I know that if I keep strengthening my faith in you this will get easier and easier. It's just so hard sometimes. All the kids at school are so totally consumed with how they look. I want to look good, but I don't want to obsess over it. Please help me find this place within me where I can look my best and be my best. With faith in you, Lord, I know I can do it!

**Amen**

button-down shirt with pressed jeans. His hair is cut short and always stays his natural color. On the weekends you can usually find John wherever the action is. If kids are drinking and doing drugs, you can bet he's at the front of the line. He seldom studies, and his grades are so bad his parents are worried about whether or not he'll get accepted to college. Easy point to make, huh?

So, does God care how we dress? Of course not! God looks at our hearts. And we should be careful not to judge others by how they are dressed, especially if they are dressed

> ## WISE WORDS
>
> BEWARE OF ALL ENTERPRISES THAT REQUIRE NEW CLOTHES, AND NOT RATHER A NEW WEARER OF CLOTHES. IF THERE IS NOT A NEW MAN, HOW CAN THE NEW CLOTHES BE MADE TO FIT? IF YOU HAVE ANY ENTERPRISE BEFORE YOU, TRY IT IN YOUR OLD CLOTHES.
>
> HENRY DAVID THOREAU, *THOREAU ON MAN AND NATURE*

differently from us due to cultural or financial differences. The Lord expects us to accept each other for who we are inside—not for how we're dressed. But does he expect us to dress appropriately when the situation calls for it? Absolutely!

## IT'S A TEST!

Tools: magazines, scissors, glue, construction paper, markers

What to Do:
Cut out pictures of people in all walks of life, dressed in a wide variety of clothes. Glue each picture to a square of construction paper. Assign each person an occupation from this list (write it on the back of the picture): doctor, vet, pastor, teacher, drug dealer, homeless shelter volunteer, secretary, nurse. (Make sure your choices are unexpected judging from appearance!)

The Game: Pass around the pictures, and have everyone guess what the person does for a living. Then turn over the picture and see the correct answer.

The Point: Discuss what kinds of prejudicial judgments you tend to make about people based on their appearance!

### BIBLE BITS & BYTES

The tallest man in the Bible was Goliath; he was a Philistine giant. The Bible says Goliath measured "six cubits and a span," or about 9½ feet tall. King Solomon was also tall; the Bible says he stood "head and shoulders above everyone else."

> YOU CAN EXPRESS YOURSELF AND STILL BE APPROPRIATE FOR THE SITUATION.

## PRAYING FOR PURPOSE

> " The trouble with you is that you make your decisions on the basis of appearance. You must recognize that we belong to Christ just as much as those who proudly declare that they belong to Christ. "
> 2 CORINTHIANS 10:7 NLT

**Dear Father in heaven,** Help me not judge people by their outward appearance, and let me be comfortable with and accepting of everyone. I've got a lot to learn about this, Father, and I need your help. I know it's not right to judge, and yet it's hard to stop myself. It's like it's an automatic response. I  trust in you and believe in you above all else, and I know that it's not right to react to people in this way.

I pray that, with your help and guidance, I may learn to accept everyone for who they are and how they look. Thank you, Father. This I pray in your name, **Amen**

# What if My Friends Make Fun of My Faith?

> Remember the word that I said to you, 'Servants are not greater than their master.' If they persecuted me, they will persecute you.
>
> JOHN 15:20

In high school, I had a friend who used to tell Jesus jokes in front of me. His favorite was about how Jesus tried to walk on water after the resurrection, but he sank because of the holes in his feet. (Yeah, I know... *not* funny!) I never laughed at those jokes, but he did.

My friend wasn't a Christian. He told those jokes to get a rise out of me. But I don't think he realized how much the jokes hurt me. He was belittling Jesus. Jesus means a lot to me. My friend was picking on the most important member of my family, and he might as well have been picking on me.

Maybe you know people like my high school friend. Perhaps you've been picked on for your faith. If so, you know how upsetting it can be. No one enjoys getting singled-out and treated with disrespect. It hurts. While we can't stop people from making fun of us or of our Christian faith, we can gain some valuable perspective that might help us deal with it.

Jesus warned his disciples that they would face the same kind of persecution he did. Jesus was run out of town by an angry mob, rejected in his hometown as a show-off, criticized by religious leaders, betrayed by Judas, denied by Peter, and eventually mocked, whipped, and crucified by the Romans for all the political trouble he was stirring up in Jerusalem. And we know from church tradition that most of the disciples were also executed for their faith—just as Jesus warned.

In the United States, we aren't familiar with that kind of treatment. We have the freedom to practice whatever religion we want—America's founders made sure of that; they themselves came here to escape religious persecution. But there are many parts of the world, even today, where people are put in prison, beaten, and even killed because they're Christians. Unless we're missionaries to those parts of the world, we'll never have to face such terrible persecution. (Puts our own troubles in perspective, huh?)

Even though we aren't being stoned in the streets for believing in Christ, we

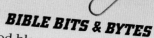
should still be prepared for the kind of persecution we face on a daily basis. It takes nothing more than turning on a television to see that Christians here are sometimes ridiculed, picked on, looked down on, harassed, and disrespected. And while you can't prevent it from happening, how you handle it will say a lot about who you are—and who Jesus is!

The following list should help you the next time you're getting picked on.

• *Remember that Jesus said it would happen.* It happened to Jesus first, then to millions of believers who came after him. You're in good company when you're harassed for your faith.

• *Remember Christians in other countries who are in prison and dying for their faith.* Whenever someone picks on you for your faith, remember the people who have it a lot worse than you. Pray that God will strengthen them, and thank God that you don't face the same treatment.

• *Remember that they "know not what they are doing," and pray for them.* Jesus prayed that God would forgive those who were crucifying him. He also prayed that God would forgive those who were harassing him as he died on a cross. Jesus knew they did not understand who he was. And the people who make fun of you don't know any better, either. So treat them with patience and love instead of anger and resentment.

• *Meet with other Christians for support.* There's strength in numbers; you don't have to face persecution alone. Share your struggles, and pray for each other. (You'll probably wind up making some great friends, too!)

**Dear Jesus,**
It's a relief to know you understand how it feels to be made fun of. I'm glad I can count on you to be with me whenever it happens. Even when my friends let me down by saying mean things, I know that you'll always be faithful to me. That helps me not worry so much about what other people think of me. Thank you for helping me. I love you, Jesus!
**Amen**

## *Solo Time*

Read Mark 14:3–9. The woman in this passage is expressing her love for Jesus. The people around her think she's being foolish, and they try to embarrass her.

How do you think she feels as people are making fun of her?

A:

What does Jesus say in her defense?

A:

How do you think she feels after Jesus defended her?

A:

Why do you think Jesus said, "Wherever the good news is proclaimed in the whole world, what she has done will be told in remembrance of her"?

A:

When we get picked on because of our faith, we can be sure that Jesus is our defender. He's right there with us saying, "Good job! I'm so proud of how you love me!"

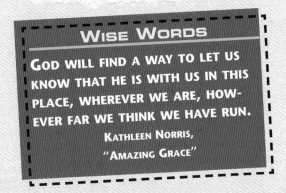

# PRAYING FOR PURPOSE

**Dear Jesus,**

It's hard to deal with people making fun of me and of you, Jesus. I have enough on my plate without defending my faith, too. But I admit that sometimes I don't take a stand for my faith because I don't want my friends thinking I'm weird. Forgive me for wanting to hide what I believe. I guess sometimes  I'm pretty weak. But I do want to stand up for you. I don't want to fear what people might say if they know I'm a Christian.

Help me, Jesus, to walk in faith every day. It helps to know that you said persecution would happen to me and that what you went through was way worse than anything I'm going through. Help me love the people who make fun of me for my faith. Help me be a witness to them for you. In your name I pray, **Amen**

# What Would God Think of Rap?

A lot of us think we have lousy memories. History dates and geometry theorems go in and out of our brains with remarkable ease. We can stare for hours at a list of facts that need to be memorized and still draw a blank when we have the test paper in front of us. We can hear the homeroom teacher say, "Okay, class, listen up. These

announcements are important." We perk up and try to pay attention, but ten seconds after she's finished we don't have a clue what the announcements were about. Our parents say, "Hey. Did my business partner call with a really important message for me last night?" We dimly reply, "Maybe. I remember someone called about something."

Why is that? Are we just memory challenged? Did the memory gene skip a generation when it came to us? It may be nice to think we are somehow incapable of memorizing anything—that way it's not our fault if we forget. But, I'm afraid, that is usually not the case.

Want proof? Get in a conversation with some friends where someone sings a stupid commercial jingle. Before you know it, dozens of absolutely absurd commercial songs are popping into your head. Unfortunately, the dumbest one will stay with you for the next six weeks.

## THINK! THINK! THINK!

PROBABLY THE SIMPLEST WAY TO KEEP YOURSELF FROM BEING SHAPED BY THE MEDIA IN WAYS THAT AREN'T POSITIVE IS JUST TO THINK. WHEN YOU WATCH A MOVIE, ASK YOURSELF "WHAT IS THIS SAYING ABOUT RELATIONSHIPS, SEX, OR LIFE THAT IS POSITIVE? WHAT IS IT SAYING THAT'S NEGATIVE?" WHEN YOU LISTEN TO MUSIC, ASK "WHAT IS THIS SONG SAYING? WHAT IS THE SINGER TRYING TO COMMUNICATE?" JUST BY EVALUATING THE MEDIA AROUND YOU, YOU CAN CONTROL THE IMPACT IT HAS ON YOU.

Or have you had this experience? You listen to the radio and hear a song you haven't heard in a few years. Before you know it, without even thinking about it, you are singing along with every word of the song. Even though you can't remember any plot lines from any of the Shakespeare plays you've had to read for school, I'll bet you have all of your favorite show memorized, and that you can quote scene for scene most of the episodes.

Let's face it. The music we listen to and the things we watch on TV and in the movies stick in our brains like nothing else. Those words and melodies and images become a part of us—they last. We often don't even have to try to remember them or recall them, and yet we find that months or years later we can remember every word or image.

**BUMPER STICKER THEOLOGY**

**WWJW. WHAT WOULD JESUS WATCH?**

**My Lord in heaven,**

Life can be so confusing! I'm so thankful you have given us the power to make our own choices. I just pray to you that I have the ability to make good ones! Please guide me as I make my way through these difficult times. I know you have a path laid out for me; help me see the right way to turn at every crossroad.

I also pray to be able to help others make good choices. I know I sometimes have influence over my friends' decisions, and I want to be able to show them your light and help them walk on the proper path. I just don't want to come on too strong or preachy. Help me know just what to do and when—help me find the proper words to have a positive impact.

Thank you, Lord, for letting me follow your light.

**Amen**

This can be either a helpful or disturbing part of our quest to live a Christian life with purpose. We'd often like to think that what we watch and listen to is merely innocent entertainment, that it has no impact upon the person we are becoming. The reality is that everything we watch or listen to, especially things we see or hear repeatedly, becomes part of what contributes to who we are and how we think about the world.

If we listen to a steady stream of music that has profanity, it will be hard for us to avoid using that language in our own conversation. Not to say it's impossible, but it's hard. If we watch lots of violent or highly sexual images, our thoughts will begin to be influenced by those images. If we watch a movie that models acts of sacrificial love or heroic courage, it becomes easier for us to see ourselves living that kind of life.

That said, there are times when it can be important to view things that might be violent or have rough content. For instance, several years ago the movie *Schindler's List* came out. It showed pretty graphic representations of Nazi atrocities toward the Jews during World War II. It wasn't a fun movie to watch, but for many people, watching it was an important and helpful means to understand the horror of the Holocaust and the need to ensure nothing like that ever happens again. And there are times when listening to an angry rap song might help us understand the social injustices and situations that lead to that anger.

There's no way to draw a strict line and say, "If you hear X number of profanities in your music, you'll then begin to talk that way yourself," or "If you watch Y number of acts of violence, you'll begin to think and perhaps even act that

Hey Steve,

One of my Christian friends comes from a family that never listens to pop music or watches movies that aren't rated G. That seems awfully strict to me. Do all Christians need to take such a conservative approach? Should I throw out my CD collection?

Music Lover

Dear Music,

The Bible says a few things that can be helpful for us as we think about our approach to the culture around us. On the one hand, there are clear instructions to live pure lives and to avoid things that make that harder for us to do. On the other hand, there are times when followers of Jesus differed on what distracted them from following God. Christianity started in the Roman world in a culture that offered animals as sacrifices to pagan gods. Those animals were later sold as meat at the local market. Some Christians thought it was idolatry to eat that meat while others thought that since they hadn't been part of the idol worship, didn't believe in it, and just wanted a good roast, it was okay to buy that meat at the market. On that issue, the Bible said each Christian needed to follow their own conscience.

I'd say the same thing applies to you and your friend. You should respect his conviction that he shouldn't listen to pop music. At the same time, he should respect your listening habits. It is important for you to consider what you aren't willing to listen to, however. You may not draw as strict a line as your friend, but you should have standards for yourself as a follower of Jesus. Good luck.

way." The point I'm trying to make is, the more we watch and listen to things that are positive and wholesome and that show people treating other people with respect, the easier it will be for us to be that kind of person. The more we watch and listen to things that are violent or obscene, the harder it will be to resist being influenced by them.

Think about the second part of the opening Bible passage. If a friend comes over and sees that you have Eminem in your CD player, what are you saying? Is that the example you want to set?

All entertainment is not bad, and there is lots that we can watch that is really fun. We do, however, need to keep an eye and an ear toward the images we subject ourselves to; we must understand that they are more a part of us than we realize. After all, I've got an annoying commercial jingle rumbling around in my head; if it's in there, who knows what else is!

## WHAT ELSE IS THERE TO DO?

It might be hard to imagine, but there are things you can do—by yourself and with friends—that actually don't even involve films, music, or video games! Really!

Next time you're stuck about whether or not to go to that R-rated horror movie, how about trying one of these instead? (We've started the list—you add to it!)

1. Board games
2. Conversation
3. Bike ride
4.
5.
6.
7.
8.

## NO SEX, DRUGS, OR ROCK 'N' ROLL

Sometimes it seems that everywhere we turn there is something that isn't good for us: a television show with too much sex, a rap song about drugs and sex, a video game loaded with violence. It's nearly impossible to avoid seeing or hearing some of this stuff.

So, the thing to keep in mind is: Can I watch and still make good choices for myself?

## SHARE WITH THE GROUP!

Did that episode of *Friends* that dealt with out-of-wedlock pregnancy teach you something?

Get together with good friends who share your concerns about the media. Everyone should bring an example to share about a song, or movie, or whatever seems inappropriate but taught them something.

Start the popcorn popping, and begin the discussion!

## PRAYING FOR PURPOSE

> **Whatever you eat or drink or whatever you do, you must do all for the glory of God. Don't give offense to Jews or Gentiles or the church of God. That is the plan I follow, too. I try to please everyone in everything I do. I don't just do what I like or what is best for me, but what is best for them so they may be saved.**
>
> **1 CORINTHIANS 10:31-33 NLT**

**Dear God,**

You are the author of stories and the composer of songs. I thank you for the world of books, music, and movies and all the good they can do and the joy they can bring. I pray that you will help me have a discerning heart to the things I listen to and watch.

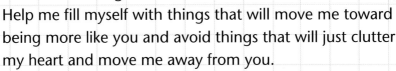

Help me fill myself with things that will move me toward being more like you and avoid things that will just clutter my heart and move me away from you.

**Amen**

# What if My Family Doesn't Share My Faith?

*Let your light shine before others, so that they may see your good works and give glory to your Father in heaven.*

**MATTHEW 5:16**

Sandy had worked hard for years to strengthen her faith and get closer to God. She was very active in her church's youth activities, was close friends with her youth pastor, and regularly attended Sunday services. Sandy had learned about God and her religion from her family when she was little. Back then, her mother had insisted on church every Sunday, even when Sandy and her Dad would beg for "a day off" as her Dad put it. Then as Sandy got older, she began to notice that *she* was the one pushing her parents to go to church on Sundays. Her Dad always wanted to sleep in, and her Mom would claim she had too many chores to attend to. Eventually, once

## BUMPER STICKER THEOLOGY

**FAITH MEANS BELIEVING EVEN WHEN IT SEEMS YOU'RE THE ONLY ONE.**

she could drive herself, Sandy stopped trying to get them to come with her, and they just quit going. Now she goes by herself every Sunday. It makes her

## LET'S ASK STEVE!

Dear Steve:

My stepmom is Buddhist, my Dad is Jewish, and I'm a Christian (like my mom). I live with my Dad now because my Mom moved to take a job out of town. Life is just getting too, too confusing and complicated. What am I supposed to do? How do I handle this? Who can I talk to? Help!

Confused Faith

Dear Confused,

You're living in a virtual world religions class! Cool! But confusing, yes, I understand. You can handle this, though. And you know how? With your faith and prayer and the help of your Lord, Jesus. It's important that you go to church and participate in all the ways you love. And it's also important that you respect and honor your parents and their individual traditions. And pray for them. When you need to talk, try talking to your pastor. But don't forget that your dad and stepmom are also there for you. Just don't try to change their religious views. Instead share with them how important your faith is to you, and let them know what you're thinking about. If they are doing something that makes it hard for you to follow your faith, share that with them—and work together with them to straighten it out. You'll come out of this with a much greater understanding of other religions than most people! And be glad and thankful that your dad and stepmother have a faith.

really sad that her parents don't share her faith, and she also worries about them. If Jesus doesn't have a presence in their lives, what will become of them?

Sandy's story, in one form or another, isn't that uncommon. Lots of us have families that don't share our faith. Sometimes there are family members who are a different faith altogether; some are believers in Christ, but they just don't ever get to church. Others simply have no faith—no religion—nothing that they believe in.

So, there you are, trying with all your strength, all your heart, all your soul to live a life filled with your faith and love of God, but your family is in a totally different place. What do you do? Well, you keep up with *your* faith and beliefs. And that includes praying for your whole family, no matter what they do or don't believe.

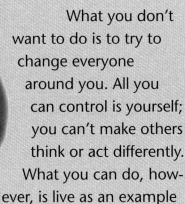

What you don't want to do is to try to change everyone around you. All you can control is yourself; you can't make others think or act differently. What you can do, however, is live as an example of the life and the faith you believe in. What you do speaks way louder than anything you might say. In simply living your life with God, you might sway an opinion or two!

Be sure to do an attitude adjustment on yourself every now and again. A superior attitude can creep up on you when you're not paying attention, and it's a real turnoff. You have found the life and the faith that is right for you; it's not up to you to dictate what is right for someone else. You can pray for them and hope they find salvation, but don't act like you're better than someone else. It turns them away, and it leads you away from the life you are trying to lead.

It's tough when your family doesn't share your faith. Remember to count all the blessings you *do* share with your family. Keep your faith and keep praying, and the Lord will be there for you!

> **BELIEVE** WHAT YOUR HEART TELLS YOU TO BELIEVE, **ACT** AS IF EVERYTHING DEPENDS ON FAITH, AND **PRAY** FOR ALL OF US ON THIS EARTH.

Hear me, O God,
    as I pray for myself,
    as I pray for my family,
    as I pray for all people everywhere.
Hear me, O God,
    as I lift my eyes to you
    and ask that you watch over me
    and my family
    and all people.
Hear me, O God,
    guide and protect me
    and everyone in my family.
Keep us holy,
    each in our own way,
    and keep us all moving in the
    right direction.
Hear me, O God,
    and keep us all standing
    in the light of your watchful eye
    as we go about our lives.
Thank you, God,
    for listening and for loving.
Amen

# PRAYING FOR PURPOSE

**Dear Lord,**

I'm very worried about my family. And I guess I'm worried about me, too.

You know that I believe in you with my whole heart and soul. I'm really trying hard to devote my life to fulfilling your purpose for me here on earth. I pray a lot and try so hard to listen for the ways you want me to turn. I just don't understand why I should be in a family that doesn't share my faith. Why, Lord? I don't mean to question your wisdom, and yet it's in my nature to question most everything. I mean, there are so many kids who don't have the kind of faith that I do. Why couldn't they have a family of nonbelievers?

Of course, I love my family, Lord. They are wonderful, and I wouldn't trade them for anyone or anything. They love me, too. And I know they try hard to provide me with a good and loving home. And just like I don't understand their lack of faith, I don't think they understand my total and complete faith.

So, please help us, Lord. Help me love my family as they are and not question your ways. I will continue praying for them, hoping they find their way to you, to learn to love you and have faith in you as I do. And please help us get along and remember how blessed we are to have each other. This I pray with my whole heart.

**Amen**

# Should I Date Only Christians?

" Above all else, guard your heart,
for it is the wellspring of life. "
PROVERBS 4:23 NIV

Dating should come with a warning label: "Proceed with caution! Dating the opposite sex has been known to cause severe heart trauma, nausea, sleeplessness, and headaches!" If you've ever been on the dating roller coaster, you know what I mean. And even if you've just dreamed of dating the guy or girl of your dreams, you know how depressing it can be waiting for that special someone to come along. So how can you navigate the confusing—and often painful—world of dating and grow closer to God at the same time? It isn't easy, but I'd like to share with you some of the wisdom I've gained from my less-than-stellar dating past.

• *No other person will ever be able to fully satisfy your hungry heart.* We all want to be loved in a special way. But God never meant for our dating relationships

*Dear Jenny,*

*I'm 17, and I've never had a real girlfriend. I'm starting to feel like a reject. I try to believe that God will have somebody for me someday. But all that girls seem to want from me is someone to talk to when they get dumped. And as soon as they find another guy to date, I'm history. I don't understand. What can I do to make girls realize that I can be more than just a friend?*
*Lonely in Lansing*

Dear Lonely,

I know this may be hard to believe, but in just a few short years a lot of those girls will want a guy just like you! When they learn—after much heartbreak—how important it is to date a guy who respects them and treats them well, they'll be on the hunt for you! Until then, use this time to learn how to be an even better friend to those girls. (It sounds like they need your shoulder to cry on!) It'll be great practice for the day when God brings you some-one special.

One more thing: Have you con-sidered that God may want you dateless right now? It's true we all want to be loved. God understands that. But maybe if God gave you the girlfriend you want right now, you'd spend more time with her than with him. And God never wants second place in our hearts. My advice is to also spend this time getting closer to God. Even as you wait for him to bring a special girl into your life, he's building your faith in him. Trust him. Go to him with your loneliness. You'll be better for it and so will your future special girl!

to take his place in our lives. I have a wonderful Christian spouse who loves me more than I ever dreamed I could be loved. But guess what? I still get lonely sometimes. As great as a spouse may be, they can't be our "everything." Only Jesus can be that.

• *"Missionary dating" is a bad idea.* No, I don't mean dating a missionary! I mean that dating a non-Christian, hoping your witness will turn him or her to Jesus, is a bad idea. A *very* bad idea. In 2 Corinthians 6:14–15 (NLT), the Bible says, "Don't team up with those who are unbelievers. How can goodness be a partner with wickedness? How can light live with darkness? What harmony can there be between Christ and the Devil? How can a believer be a partner with an unbeliever?" Dating is tough territory even with another committed Christian—but imagine how much tougher it is when the person you're dating doesn't care about Jesus and what you believe! You may think you're strong enough to handle it. But if God warns against it, shouldn't you take him seriously? After all, God knows you better than you know yourself, right?

• *A watched pot never boils.* Let's face it, it's hard to walk down the halls at school and see a couple looking at each other all goo-goo eyed and draped over one another. And there are lots of couples! Of course you wonder,

"Hey! What's wrong with me? How come I don't have somebody special? When is it gonna be my turn?" And usually some well-intentioned adult says, "It never happens when you're looking for it. It'll happened when you least expect it!" Ugh! I hate to say it, but most of the time it's true! (I met my spouse at a convention for youth pastors. I was there to lead a seminar about being *single* in youth ministry. God sure has a sense of humor!)

If you spend all your time wishing someone will come along, you'll waste a lot of time. Instead, use that time to enjoy your friends and have fun. Take your dating desert and turn it into an oasis where you spend time focusing on your relationship with God! If you do, you'll be more than ready when God gives you that special someone.

• *It's okay to be single.* In a world where people are constantly hooking up, it can seem like you're the only weird one in the bunch. Truthfully, it can be lonely. I know, I was 30 when I got married. Most of my friends were already married and had children by that point. But being single gave me a chance to get closer to God. And though it was a challenge being single in a world full of couples, I'm glad I had that time in my life. So, don't listen to the lie that says you're missing out if you aren't dating. It just isn't true.

• *Give God control of your dating life.* You might already know what happens when you don't listen to God in the area of relationships. You wind up going too far physically and regretting it. You wind up dating someone who isn't good for you and draws you away from God instead of closer to him. Or you wind up losing yourself in a suffocating relationship. God has something so much better for you. He wants you to have positive and healthy relationships with the opposite sex. Trust him with this important area of your life. God will never steer you wrong!

## PRAYING FOR PURPOSE

**Dear God,**
Sometimes it's hard to wait for that special someone. I want you to hurry up and give me a relationship so I don't have to be alone anymore. But help me be patient and use this time to get closer to you. I don't want anyone to take your place in my heart. And I know that having a relationship won't make me truly happy. Only you can do that. Remind me whenever I feel discouraged or lonely to go to you. Please give me good friends to have fun with. Help me use this time in my life to grow into the person you've created me to be. In Jesus' name I pray,
**Amen**

# Drugs: Is the Bible Silent?

❝ **Happy are those who do not follow the advice of the wicked, or take the path that sinners tread, or sit in the seat of scoffers; but their delight is in the law of the Lord, and on his law they meditate day and night.** ❞
**PSALM 1:1-2**

The Bible. The Good Book. It's our, well, it's our "bible" that guides us through life. It's our "everything book." It teaches, explains, and helps us understand God and the world. It's an amazing book with

answers to some of life's toughest questions. Its purpose is to help us understand the Lord, ourselves, and each other. It is there to help us learn to live the kind of life that he wants us to live and to follow the path that he has chosen for us.

**Dear Lord,**

Please help me be strong and avoid the temptation of drugs. I know people who are into drugs, and I know they are sinning. They are destroying the body you gave them, and they are acting in ways that aren't cool. Help me stay away from them and their temptations. Help me remember everything I am striving for—to be a believer and to walk in your light, to be a good student, to be the kind of kid my parents will be proud of. Help me stick by my choices. I don't want to do something I could regret for the rest of my life. Please help me, Lord. Stand by me, and help me believe in my ability to make good choices with your help. Thank you, Lord.

**Amen**

And what do we do if we have a particular question or issue that is not specifically addressed in the Bible? Do we abandon it for something more modern? Do we announce that we have stumped the Bible? Do we assume that if something isn't expressly forbidden, it's okay? Do we say it's time to stop asking questions and start finding answers?

It does, at first glance, appear that the Bible is indeed silent on the issue of drugs.

## DISCUSS IT!

GET TOGETHER WITH A GROUP OF FRIENDS, AND TALK ABOUT WHAT YOU THINK JESUS WOULD DO IF HE WAS OFFERED DRUGS. THINK ABOUT IT. HOW CAN YOUR ANSWERS HELP YOU TO BE BETTER PREPARED TO WALK AWAY IF YOU ARE OFFERED DRUGS?

# PURPOSEFUL PONDERABLE

❝ Do you not know that you are God's temple and that God's spirit dwells in you? ❞

**1 CORINTHIANS 3:16**

You are a temple of God, made in his image. You strive to be close to God, and he is part of you. His spirit actually dwells within all of us. So if God's spirit is inside you, you want to treat your body as something sacred. That means taking good care of yourself inside and out—pure thoughts, no drugs, no alcohol, no sex. So even though the Bible doesn't specifically say *not* to do something, it's pretty easy to figure out what's a good way to treat your body and what isn't.

But, as with most issues, if we investigate further, we can find enough information to draw some pretty clear conclusions of what the Lord has in mind on the subject! We can find references to the Lord being a part of everyone who believes in him. His spirit lives within us, so we know that we need to take loving care of ourselves.

We tend to the well-being of our spirits through our religious observances, our faith, and

## BUMPER STICKER THEOLOGY

### JWDD! (JESUS WOULDN'T DO DRUGS!)

```
D ON'T
R ISK
U NDERMINING EVERYTHING.
G OD IS
S TANDING BY!
```

our prayers. He also expects that we will treat our bodies with the utmost respect through proper nutrition, adequate rest and exercise, and abstaining from the use of any substance that is physically harmful or alters our good sense. We are also taught to refrain from any activity that could harm others.

Drugs harm not only the user, both physically and emotionally, but all his or her friends and family are affected as well. When someone abuses drugs or

### BIBLE BITS & BYTES

My child, if sinners entice you, do not consent. If they say, "Come with us, let us lie in wait for blood; let us wantonly ambush the innocent; like Sheol let us swallow them alive and whole, like those who go down to the Pit. We shall find all kinds of costly things; we shall fill our houses with booty. Throw in your lot among us; we will all have one purse"— my child, do not walk in their way, keep your foot from their paths.

Proverbs 1:10–15

alcohol, there is always the potential of doing unintentional harm to others.

There are also references to the evils of drinking, and we know that drugs can also cause damage to our bodies, minds, and souls. The Bible tells us not to blindly follow those who do evil acts. This warns us not to follow others into activities we know are wrong.

So, check it out! If there's something that affects your life, you can bet the Bible isn't actually silent. It just might mean you have to study it carefully and then listen with your heart!

★ ◉ ★

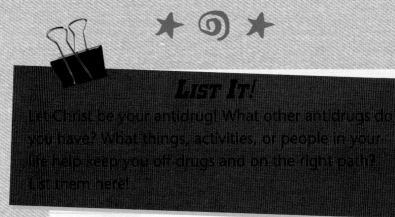

### LIST IT!

List Christ be your antidrug! What other antidrugs do you have? What things, activities, or people in your life help keep you off drugs and on the right path? List them here!

1.
2.
3.
4.
5.

Then add one sentence about each one; describe why they're such an awesome antidrug.

## PRAYING FOR PURPOSE

> **Because he himself was tested by what he suffered, he is able to help those who are being tested.**
> **HEBREWS 2:18**

**Dear Jesus,**

I pray that I will always make good, healthy choices in this beautiful life you have given me. I trust that I know in my heart what is right and what is wrong. I have faith that you will help me stay on the path of good choices.

I pray that I will take good care of my body, my spirit, and my soul—these incredible gifts that you have given me. Please help my friends see that staying healthy and off drugs is the best way—the only way. Thank you for your guidance and your love.

**Amen**

# I've Got the Headache, so Where's the High Life?

> ❝ I came that they may have life, and have it abundantly. ❞
>
> **JOHN 10:10**

Over the centuries, Christianity has looked down on drinking alcohol, but Jesus drank wine. Why are so many churches hung up on not drinking? Maybe, if we take a look at why people drink, and particularly why they drink heavily, it might make a little more sense to us.

Few people drink excessively because

a) they just love the taste of six or seven beers

b) they really like the sensation of stumbling around, falling down, and vomiting

c) they get very excited about the prospect of waking up the next morning feeling like a 300-piece marching band is playing inside their heads

d) they like being so dehydrated they feel a kinship to the Sahara.

> **COMPARISON SHOPPING**
>
> WATCH A FEW SPORTING EVENTS ON TV THIS WEEKEND. MAKE A LIST OF ALL THE PROMISES BEER COMMERCIALS MAKE. THEN ASK YOURSELF, "WHAT DELIVERS ON THEIR PROMISES BETTER, BEER OR GOD?"

If those aren't reasons why people drink a ton, why do they do it?

For one thing, we all really want to be liked. If we went to schools where it seemed like the best way to have lots of friends was to be heavily into chess or crossword puzzles, most of us would be busy working on our gaming skills. We want to be accepted by the crowd. But at many schools, it seems that the crowd is lined up around the beer keg.

We also are people who want to be confident, relaxed, and carefree. But most of us are self-conscious, a little uptight, and kind of stressed out. We might think we'd be more outgoing and comfortable if we had a few drinks. We may think, *I know it's not really me, but at least it looks like me.*

Finally, sometimes we want an escape. It might be escape from the pressures we feel to perform, escape from fears and worries we have, or escape from disappointing or painful situations in our lives. We all feel the need for some relief at times. The problem is that when we're drunk, our cares and worries haven't really gone anywhere. But, for a while at least, we can't feel them.

I'm convinced Jesus wouldn't walk into the big party this weekend and start pointing his finger and calling people sinners. I do think he would walk around for a while and feel really sad. He'd walk up to some folks and ask, "Do you really think this is the only way people will like you? I think you are so inter-

> **THINK.**
> **DON'T DRINK.**

esting and awesome just as you are. You don't have to do things you don't really even like." To another group he'd say, "So this is what you think fun is? I know what you're like when you are sober, and you're hilarious. Right now you barely make sense, and you're just obnoxious and rude." Finally, he'd stop by some to say, "I know you're hurting. While the pain goes away for a few hours, don't you know it will be right back tomorrow—and will be even worse? Don't you want comfort that will last?"

I don't think Jesus would frown on drinking because it's evil. I think he would frown upon it because it is often a cheap substitute for what we are really looking for. We want friends who are friends because of who we are, not what we are willing to do. We want to be fun, outgoing, and relaxed on our own; we want that to be who we really are, not just how we are when we're loaded. We want comfort for life's hurts and worries, not a painkiller that wears off in an hour or two. We need something that will be there the day after the party.

Jesus wants us to have great fun and fabulous friendships. Why settle for a cheap imitation that lasts a few hours and leaves us feeling awful? Jesus wants us to have fun that is meaningful and filled with purpose. Don't settle for less.

# LET'S ASK STEVE!

*Hey Steve,*

*I am a junior in high school and play on a lot of sports teams at my school. On weekends most of my teammates and a lot of kids I know throw parties where there might be drinking. These are my friends, but I don't want to drink. Do I have to just sit at home? Am I going to have to give up my convictions to have friends?*

*Tired of Watching TV Alone on Friday Night*

Dear Tired,

Here are a few suggestions that might help your situation. First, if the party is unsupervised by responsible adults, don't go. Go to the next paragraph. If there is adult supervision, find a friend who has the same views on drinking as you do, has the same group of friends, and go to the party together. Bring a six-pack of soda, and commit to backing each other up. You can be with your friends, have fun, and not drink. (Note: Always use common sense: Never get into a car with someone who has had even one drink. NEVER!) If it looks like there is drinking at the party, get out of there. It isn't a good situation to be in.

Second, you can arrange stuff to do with friends outside of situations where there may be drinking. What are other things they like to do? Make a plan, and have fun.

Finally, broaden your horizons. I bet there are lots of nondrinking, really fun kids at your school that you've never socialized with before. Look around; you might find some great new friends to add to your list of people you hang out with.

## *List It!*

There are a million (better!) ways to relax other than drinking. How about walking? Swimming? Hanging out with your dog? What works for you?

1.
2.
3.
4.
5.

## *Praying for Purpose*

> " **Wine is a mocker, strong drink a brawler, and whoever is led astray by it is not wise.** "
> **PROVERBS 20:1**

**Lord,**

Help me grow into a responsible adult when it comes to drinking. Keep me moving forward on a healthy path, able to say no to peer pressure.

Lord, I pray for your light to always guide me and that I never forget that it is my faith in you that will take me through the tough times. I know drinking will only make anything bad even worse. When I need to unwind, I pray you will lead me to call a friend, pick up my Bible, or find a safe and healthy way to relax. I know that I do not need an external substance to be myself. This I pray to you today with my whole heart.

**Amen**

# I'll Take That Hamburger Plain, Please

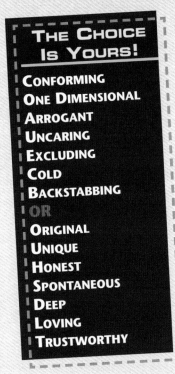

**THE CHOICE IS YOURS!**

CONFORMING
ONE DIMENSIONAL
ARROGANT
UNCARING
EXCLUDING
COLD
BACKSTABBING
OR
ORIGINAL
UNIQUE
HONEST
SPONTANEOUS
DEEP
LOVING
TRUSTWORTHY

I have to confess, when it comes to food, I'm about as plain as can be. If I'm eating pancakes, don't give me fruit toppings, powdered sugar, or whipped cream. Just hand over the maple syrup. If it's hamburgers, I might take a piece of cheese, but no thanks on the ketchup, mustard, lettuce, tomato, and pickles. When I put food on my plate, I don't mix it. I keep everything separate. I prefer to eat each item one at a time.

I know I'm in the minority on this one. Most people like to put at least a few toppings on the food they eat. Some of you probably even mix up

Hey Steve,

I've been really looking at my life lately and trying to live it the way God would like me to. That's led me to make decisions that some of my friends aren't too cool with. Am I going to have to decide between having any friends and respecting myself?

Feeling Friendless in Fresno

Dear FFIF,

At first there might be some cost to having principles. I will promise you, though, that even within the group of people that might make fun of your decisions there are those who wish they had your courage. You'll find them. You'll also find new people who share your convictions. Plus, over time, you'll make a difference. Lots of times it only takes a few people standing up for what's right (for example, not picking on people, not using drugs or alcohol) for the whole climate of a group to change. Finally, trust that God sees and smiles on your efforts. Knowing that you are pleasing him can help give you confidence when things get tough.

your food on your plate. Shocking! Then there are the folks who are my polar opposite. They don't add a little bit of this or a little bit of that to their food; they add a ton of everything!

Maybe I am too extreme in my food preferences, but I've seen people who start with a couple of pieces of bread and a slice of meat and start piling on everything in sight until they've got a monstrosity almost a foot high! Or, maybe you've seen the people at the salad bar who begin with a plate and some lettuce, but they need a wheelbarrow to get the "salad" back to their table after emptying the salad bar.

Here's what I don't get about this approach: How can you still recognize the sandwich you started with when you add so much stuff? Can you still taste the pancakes under all those toppings? At what point do you add so many toppings that the original food disappears?

What do food toppings have to do with living a purposeful life? Sometimes our lives end up looking like that unrecognizable hamburger patty buried beneath a few gallons of mustard and ketchup. We come into school as ourselves. Maybe we like sports, maybe we don't. Perhaps we take piano lessons, and we actually enjoy them! We could even be people who

### Wow, Lord!

It's incredible how you made each and every one of us unique! My question is, then why do we keep trying to be the same? I get so tired of all the pressure at school to be like everyone else. I get frustrated with my friends for trying to be something they're not.

Lord, please help me remember who I am inside and always be thankful for the life you have given me. As I follow this path of living for your purpose, I pray that I have the courage to share this message of the beauty of our uniqueness with friends in a way that they respond to. Please keep me moving in the direction you have planned for me.

Thank you, Lord.

### Amen

like to read a book in the summer. Pretty quickly though, we discover what the "in" crowd at our school likes. The pressure starts. All of us want to have friends. None of us want to feel on the outs of our social world. So it's very easy to start trying on new tastes, looks, even personalities that we think will be acceptable to the kids at school who set the standard.

The trouble is, it's not really us. Even if it works and we create a version of ourselves that is cool, this version isn't real. We treat people in ways we're not proud of, do things we know to be destructive, pretend to like things we don't.

> **BIBLE BITS & BYTES**
> Because of that cross, my interest in this world died long ago.
>
> GALATIANS 6:14 NLT

That's not the way God made us. We are created by God in unique and wonderful ways. When we have the courage to truly be ourselves, pretty cool things can happen. Sure, some shallow kids at school may deem our being true to our beliefs or our likes and dislikes as lame, but we also find people who say (maybe

whispered at first), "You know what, I think the same thing. I've always hated acting that way, or doing this, or pretending to like that." When that happens, it's followed by something amazing. We've found a genuine friend. Not one pretend personality acting like a friend with another fake personality. Nope. Two people each finding a true friend in each other.

Most people are too afraid to really pull this off. We too easily become who others tell us we should be. If you trust that God did a darn good job when he put you together and that it actually is more fun to be yourself than a fake, you'll find real friends. And you'll like who you see in the mirror every morning.

# A COLLAGE OF YOU

**What You'll Need:** old magazines, catalogs, etc.; scissors; glue; white paper or poster board

The Task: Cut out anything and everything that strikes your fancy as being you—pictures and words. Arrange them in a collage that represents you.

Don't think too much as you're doing this; the point is to be spontaneous and real. When you're done, you'll have a great reference for when you're tempted to do or be something that doesn't feel true to your inner self!

Plus, you'll have a cool picture for your room!

## PRAYING FOR PURPOSE

> **The human spirit is the lamp of the Lord, searching every inmost part.**
> **PROVERBS 20:27**

**God,**
Most days I feel like two desires are fighting it out inside me. The desire to really be myself and the person I'd like to be and the desire to fit in. I'm afraid of being lonely. Help me find friends who respect and like me for myself. Help me have the courage to stand up to the crowd when not standing up would mean compromising who I am. Most of all, help me know that you love me more than I can imagine.
**Amen**

# Lust in a Sex-Saturated World

> ❝ **Put to death, therefore, whatever belongs to your earthly nature: sexual immorality, impurity, lust, evil desires and greed, which is idolatry.** ❞
>
> **COLOSSIANS 3:5 NIV**

Lots of Christians struggle with lust. If you're one of them, you aren't alone. Some are addicted to pornography and sexual fantasies. Some feel trapped in a cycle of masturbation and guilt. Some are flirting with the line of "how far is too far," and still others are giving into temptation to have sex outside of marriage.

As Christians, we know that God wants us to remain pure and avoid lust. But that's hard to do when sexual images are all around us! Sex is there when you turn on the TV, go to the movies, pop in a music CD, surf the Internet—even when you watch a shampoo commercial! Those who struggle with lust have a difficult problem because our world makes it hard to solve. But there is help with God.

**BIBLE BITS & BYTES**
Habakkuk is a short book that asks why God allows evil to be strong. It is similar to Job, both of which are known as a *theodicies*, books that question God's justice.

*Dear Jenny,*

*I have kind of a weird problem. I'm a girl and I masturbate and I can't stop. I was always told that guys were the only ones who do this. I feel so ashamed. I know I shouldn't be doing this. And I feel even worse knowing this isn't usually a girl's problem. What's wrong with me?*

*Sincerely,*

*Ashamed and Anonymous*

Dear Ashamed and Anonymous,

Nothing is wrong with you! Whoever told you masturbation is only something guys do was wrong. It's actually more common among girls than you think. Still, you're right to be concerned about the fact that you can't stop. God doesn't want us controlled by anything other than him!

Let me ask: Do you know *why* you masturbate? Are you feeling lonely, anxious, or stressed out? If so, that could be what's triggering your struggle. Biologically speaking, the sex act is helpful at relieving stress, anxiety, and depression. The downside is that the relief sex provides is never long-lasting. As you probably already know, when sex is not in the proper context (between a man and woman in marriage), it can actually add to the isolation and loneliness you may be feeling. Masturbation can then become a vicious cycle that's hard to break. It sounds like that's where you are.

Here's my advice to you:

1) Tell yourself and believe it: You aren't a freak!

2) Find a Christian you can trust with this information and talk about it together. Sometimes just talking about it can release the shame and power it has over you.

3) Realize that God created girls as sexual beings, too...not just guys. Your desire to express yourself sexually does not make you odd or shameful. It makes you human.

4) Confess to God the hold your habit has over you. Tell God you don't want it controlling you anymore.

5) Ask God to heal the places in you that might be hurting or reaching out for love. If you don't let God heal the deepest parts of you, this struggle will be with you for a long time. Even if you get married and have an appropriate outlet for sexual satisfaction, you'll still get lonely, anxious, stressed, etc. And only God can really help you with those issues.

Before you read these practical steps you can take to deal with lust in your life, there are a couple of things you should know:

#1: *Lust is a cheap knock-off of love.* Lust is self-ish. When we lust, we care only about satisfying our own desires—and certainly not those of the person we're lusting after. But love always puts the other

IN A WORLD FILLED WITH LUST AND GREED, YOU CAN BE AN EXAMPLE OF FAITH AND PURITY IN CHRIST TO THE WORLD AND TO OTHER BELIEVERS AROUND YOU. THE SIN OF LUST IS USUALLY SOMETHING WE TRY TO HIDE; BUT IF WE'RE TO WIN OVER LUST, WE NEED THE HELP OF OUR BROTHERS AND SISTERS IN CHRIST.

person first! And here's something that may come as a surprise to you. Lust is never okay...not even in marriage! When you're married it's perfectly fine to *really, really* want to have sex with your spouse. But it's not okay to treat your spouse as an object for your own satisfaction.

#2: *Sexual desire is good—and not the same as lust.* Maybe you've been taught that sexual desires are bad. People who struggle with lust often believe that every time they have a sexual desire they're sinning. Then they ask God to take those sexual desires away so they won't have to feel guilty. But God will never do that for us, because sexual desire was created by God to be enjoyed—within marriage. So, yes, it's okay and perfectly normal to desire sex; it's *not* okay to take that desire, go to a porn site on the Internet, and imagine having sex with someone. It's a selfish act that makes an object out of another person and satisfies only yourself. (And since the "satisfaction" you receive isn't from God, it'll never truly satisfy you inside—so why even go there? It's not a loving thing to do. It's a lustful thing to do.)

Now let's turn to the practical stuff:

• Don't hate yourself because you have sexual desires. That's like hitting a baby for crying. Babies cry! If you hit them, you'll only make it worse. It's only when you cross the line from sexual desire to lustful thoughts and behavior that you're in trouble.

• The *moment* you sense that you're having sexual desires, STOP. . . and thank God he created you as a sexual being. (Thank God that being around that good-looking guy or girl gives you the tingles. It really is a cool thing.) Having a thankful attitude toward God for how he made you will keep God *with you* as you struggle against lust. Sometimes just reminding yourself of God's good plan for sex and being thankful for it will help give you the strength to say no to lust.

• Find a person you can talk with honestly about your struggle. It's a good idea for this person to be the same gender as you. Make sure this person is a Christian, too, because you'll want her or him to pray with and for you and to hold you accountable to stay pure in your thoughts and actions.

• Avoid those places, movies, TV shows, etc., that cause you to struggle. No need to make things more difficult by being around the things that trigger the struggle, right?

• Try to understand *why* you struggle with lust. It's not just about wanting sex. You were created for the thrill of intimacy in all its form—God, friends, family, and perhaps a spouse. Deep inside we all hunger for intimacy. But the cheap thrill that lust provides us is only a quick fix for that hunger—it can't ever satisfy us. That's something only God can do.

So the next time lust tries to grab you, remember what you're really hungry for is God—not sex! Go to God with your struggle and your need for intimacy. When you do, you'll find a God who understands what you're going through and who'll give you the grace to stand firm.

## *PRAYING FOR PURPOSE*

> **Clothe yourselves with the Lord Jesus Christ, and do not think about how to gratify the desires of the sinful nature.**
> **ROMANS 13:14 NIV**

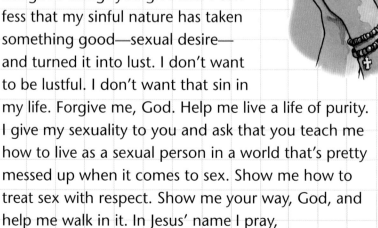

**Dear God,**
Thank you that you created me with sexual desires. But I know all too well how easy it is for me to twist the good things you give me. I confess that my sinful nature has taken something good—sexual desire— and turned it into lust. I don't want to be lustful. I don't want that sin in my life. Forgive me, God. Help me live a life of purity. I give my sexuality to you and ask that you teach me how to live as a sexual person in a world that's pretty messed up when it comes to sex. Show me how to treat sex with respect. Show me your way, God, and help me walk in it. In Jesus' name I pray,
**Amen**

# The Marriage God Designed for Us

> " If I speak in the tongues of mortals and of angels, but do not have love, I am a noisy gong or a clanging cymbal. "
>
> 1 CORINTHIANS 13:1

Marriage? I'm too young to be thinking about marriage! Why are we talking about marriage? Well, yeah, you're not anywhere near ready for marriage at this stage of life. But, admit it, you're definitely interested in looking around at the opposite sex and sort of browsing for potential partners. Not forever partners. Not marriage partners. But someone special who will help you learn about relationships and love. So the question is, what do we look for in this special person? What kind of relationship does God want us to have? Ultimately, what kind of marriage partner will the Lord lead us to?

The first thing to think about is do I have to have a boyfriend or girlfriend? The answer, we all know, is of course not! Still, sometimes it's so easy to get caught up in feeling that we just have to find someone and we have to find them now! But hey, we're talking about people here, not new shoes. You don't just run out and start shopping for a girlfriend or boyfriend. If you're buying shoes and you have to have them for a special occasion tomorrow, you might take the best fit you can find, even if you know the shoes aren't quite right. With people, though, there's never any reason to take someone who isn't quite right. You should never get into a relationship just because you want the relationship. A relationship will only work if you want the person!

Sometimes people look for another person to fill a void that is lacking in themselves. If your faith in the Lord or in yourself isn't quite up to what it should be, you might start to believe it's because you need someone else in your life to make everything whole and complete. Wrong! Don't listen to that voice! The best way to look for someone is to—are you ready?—stop looking. Focus on your faith in God and living your own life with him at the center. Step away from a selfish pre-occupation with romance. Only when you are truly living in his light, complete and content on your

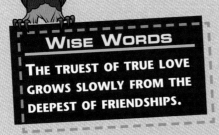

**God in heaven,**

Please help me out with all this love stuff. It's just so hard and so confusing sometimes. It seems I'm often drawn to someone who isn't good for me in one way or another. Either they don't like me back, they don't share my view of life, or they just don't want the same things I do.

God, help me see when something is wrong in a relationship so I know to back away and let it go. And please help me find what it is in me that draws me to the wrong kind of person.

I love you and believe in you, Lord, and I know you will guide me along this difficult path. I know I'm not looking for a life partner yet, just someone to care about. I know my relationships now will help me learn about love so that when I do meet my true love I will be ready to take on a lifetime commitment. Thank you, God, for all your guidance and love.

**Amen**

own, will you be ready to meet someone who is the type of person God wants you to find.

And when you are ready to meet someone, what are the qualities God designed for us? What should we look for? What should we expect? Overall, a partner should be respectful of who you are. That means you need someone in your life who is respectful of your faith, your beliefs, your deepest sense of who you are. It doesn't mean they have to agree with you on everything, but they do have to honor your

INVITATION

I DO NOT NEED SOMEONE IN MY LIFE TO COMPLETE ME; I HAVE MY LORD AND MY FAMILY AND MY FRIENDS. BUT I WOULD LIKE TO INVITE SOMEONE INTO MY LIFE WHO WILL ADD JOY TO MY DAYS AND HELP STRENGTHEN MY FAITH.

beliefs. In other words, if someone puts you down for your belief in God, then that's definitely not the partner for you!

A good way to keep tabs on this is to check out how you feel inside about this person. Do you feel free to be yourself? Do you feel you have been put down or belittled? If you find that you are changing just to please someone else, that's definitely not what God has in mind for you.

The relationship road can be rocky and volatile—there's no way out of that. But it can also be filled with caring and laughter and learning. It's not easy, but that's okay. As long as we keep God at our side, love isn't far behind.

## *HAVE YOU FOUND THE ONE?*

So you've met someone who makes your heart do backflips? Think about that person, and go through this checklist to see how many of these apply to your potential sweetie.

___ makes me laugh

___ easy to talk to

___ treats me with respect

___ respectful and polite to my parents

___ shares my faith in God

___ is faithful to me

___ is a good student

___ is a safe and responsible driver

___ is someone I can trust

___ is someone I can depend on

___ steers clear of the "wrong crowd"

___ helps me to live up to my faith

___ believes that sex should wait until marriage

___ is supportive of my activities: family functions, studying, church obligations, etc.

Any qualities left unchecked? Stop and think about it. Is that something important to you? Is it something important to God?

I asked the Lord

what true love means

and would it make me whole?

He said loves comes

straight from the heart

and fills your very soul.

He said I shouldn't

look for love

to make my life complete,

but find true meaning

in my Lord,

and then perhaps

I'll meet

someone who shares my

strength of faith

and believes in

God above.

When I'm complete

unto myself,

the Lord will send

someone to love.

## PRAYING FOR PURPOSE

> **You desire truth in the inward being; therefore teach me wisdom in my secret heart.**
> **PSALM 51:6**

Lord,

I know I've been looking for someone to help me feel complete. I pray for your guidance in learning to stop doing that. I see now that I need to feel okay on my own before I'm ready to have a strong and healthy relationship. I want to focus on my faith in you and in myself, and I know that will lead me to a place where I can find someone to share my days with in a positive way.

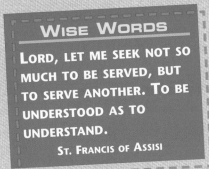

So I'll stop trying to desperately find someone. Instead I'll focus on spending each day with you, walking the path you have laid out for me.

**Amen**

# UNEXPECTED SURPRISES

> **" No eye has seen, no ear has heard, and no mind has imagined what God has prepared for those who love him. "**
>
> **1 Corinthians 2:9 NLT**

We can be pretty jaded. We know there's no Santa Claus and that the Easter Bunny isn't real. We can go through life thinking we know what's coming and not be very impressed. To that attitude, God just laughs and says, "You have no idea what wonderful stuff I'm up to!" After all, this is a God who created the vastness of space, the intricacy of human DNA, and Will Ferrell's sense of humor. These essays hardly scratch the surface of the unexpected surprises God has in store for us.

# You Are Not Alone

Just when you thought you were totally alone, guess what? Surprise! You've got a whole warehouse of resources surrounding you—you are never alone. For starters, you've got God. Now maybe he doesn't exactly sit down on the couch beside you and listen to the day's gossip after school, but you know he is with you. He is around you and within you. And he is always listening to you. You've got your parents; they're always around. (Maybe more than you'd like!) There are other family members and clergy. You've also got your friends. So even when it seems in the moment like you're all alone, you actually have a huge support network of people who will rally to the occasion.

And it's now easier than ever to get in touch with people when you feel alone—e-mail and cell phones help you do that. So even if you're not sitting beside someone, you can still be with them.

The main thing to keep in mind is that God is

with you all the time. He doesn't take a lunch break or take holidays and weekends off. He's always there. When you feel alone, try getting very quiet, calm your mind, and listen closely. See if you can sense the Lord's presence within you. With practice and prayer, you'll be able to do this anytime you need to remind yourself that he is with you.

Feeling alone is universal. Everyone experiences these emotions, so that's another way that you're certainly not alone. Talk with your friends about it, and odds are that most of them will know exactly what you're talking about because they have felt the same thing. And it's not just your friends; adults have the same feelings. So don't hesitate to talk to your parents or your pastor as well. Often you'll find that just talking about the feeling banishes it. Once you start talking about it, it's so easy to see that you really aren't alone.

Keep in mind that there is a difference between feeling lonely or empty and simply being by yourself. Spending time by yourself—alone—is a very healthy

**Lord,**

I pray that I can shake this feeling of loneliness. I love you, and I try to live a life filled with what you want me to do. I try really hard to share your message with the world and to live as an example of your goodness. I know that I don't always succeed, but I'm trying with all my heart.

I can't help wonder, then, why I always feel I'm just out here in the world totally on my own? I know you are with me, but sometimes even that doesn't help me much. Please help me find a way to feel the fullness of living according to your plan for me. Help me truly believe that your love is always with me and that the love of my family and friends is, too. Give me confidence in your love.

Lord, I don't want to feel like this anymore. Please guide me and help me get past this loneliness so I can worship you better.

**Amen**

thing to do. It's a wonderful time to pray and get closer to God. And being on your own helps make you who you are as an individual. It gives you a chance to truly spend time the way you choose and to check in with yourself to be sure you are following a path that has God at its center.

*BUMPER STICKER THEOLOGY*

**HONK IF GOD IS WITH YOU!**

Reading the Bible is a great thing to do when you're alone. It can be like having a conversation with the Lord. So don't shy away from spending time with yourself, alone. It's a good thing to do.

You are never alone in this world. You have the love of so very many, most especially your Father in heaven.

## THE WISE PERSON WITHIN

Even when you feel all alone there is much wisdom within your core that you can tap into to help you remember that you are truly loved.

Find a place that is quiet and just the right temperature. Get comfortable, and close your eyes. Visualize a place where you feel your wisdom dwells; it can be in a house, on a beach, in the mountains—anywhere that feels special to you. Breathe deeply, and ask to speak to the wise man or woman who resides deep within your soul. Ask very calmly and quietly. Do not rush. Do not be disturbed if you can't speak with this wise person at first. It may take several tries. Ask this person anything you wish to know. Anything that you have been struggling with. Be very still and quiet, and allow the wise person to talk to you and tell you the answer.

This is your wisdom—this is God's wisdom. Tap into it. Listen to its message, and remember that you are not alone.

## PRAYING FOR PURPOSE

> " Let us acknowledge the Lord; let us press on to acknowledge him. As surely as the sun rises, he will appear; he will come to us like the winter rains, like the spring rains that water the earth. "
> HOSEA 6:3 NIV

**Dear God,**
I pray for the courage and strength to spend time on my own—to not be afraid of being alone. I pray that I might find my way closer to you and to your dreams for me. I want to walk in the path you have laid out for me and fulfill the destiny that I was meant for. I know that  sometimes I shy away from being on my own; it's just that I don't like being lonely. Help me, I pray, to always remember that I'm never alone. I know in my heart that you are with me and that there are so many other people who care about me. Thank you for caring about me, Lord.
**Amen**

# God Has Good Plans for You

" There is surely a future hope
for you, and your hope will
not be cut off. "
PROVERBS 23:18 NIV

An 8th grade boy I knew shot himself. His father found him dead in their basement with a shotgun and an open Bible by his side. His suicide note read, "I'm bad. No one can forgive me. Not even God. I'm sorry."

This story still punches me in the gut even though it happened almost 16 years ago. It was a horrible, senseless death. No doubt it still haunts his family: *What would have become of him? Would he have gotten married? Had children? What kind of job would he have had?* His family will never know. All because he decided that life and God had nothing good to offer him.

You see, this boy believed the lie that he was worthless and unforgivable. Even worse, he believed the lie that God had nothing good for him: no forgiveness, no love, no future, no hope.

And worst of all, he was reading the Bible before he committed suicide. The Bible! That means he was actually reaching out to God—but he gave up. And while God was reaching out, too, something prevented this boy from hearing God's voice and the truth of his love. He couldn't hear that God had good plans for him. He couldn't believe the message of hope. Why?

We will never know what went on in his heart and mind before he pulled the trigger and gave up on life. One thing is certain: Someone lied to him and told him that life wasn't worth living. And that voice was very persuasive.

The Bible tells us that Satan prowls around like a lion looking for someone he can devour (1 Peter 5:8). Satan is pretty smart. He knows we humans are prone to question the love and forgiveness of God—especially when we're facing tough times.

Satan would like us all to believe that God is a liar. That God doesn't really love us. That God won't forgive our biggest sins. That God wouldn't waste his good plans on us. So, we have to choose which voice we're going to listen to: God's or Satan's. That day in the basement, my friend chose to listen to Satan's voice, and then he lost all chance for good things in life.

Who are you listening to? Do you hear positive messages about your future or negative ones? Are you dogged by discouragement and depression? Or do you hear God whispering messages of hope? You may not be considering suicide, but we all have times when we're discouraged about our lives and wonder what God is up to. And God

## BIBLE BITS & BYTES

I know the plans I have for you, says the Lord, plans for your welfare and not for harm, to give you a future with hope.

JEREMIAH 29:11

understands. He doesn't lose patience with us. But every day we must make the choice to listen to God's voice of love instead of Satan's voice of lies. God wants us to listen to his voice. Not Satan's.

On a personal note: I know that some of you reading this *are* thinking about suicide... or you've at least thought of it once or twice. I did, too, especially when I was in high school. (I called my sophomore year my "suffer more" year!) There were times when I came dangerously close to listening to Satan's lies. But something told me to believe that God really did have good plans for me. I am so glad I chose to listen to God's voice.

Don't get me wrong—I've had my share of bumps and bruises. But God has been faithful. If I had listened to Satan, I wouldn't be here today to enjoy my life. And you wouldn't be reading this devotional, because I wouldn't have been here to write it!

So if you are thinking about giving up on life, please know how much Jesus loves you. Please, don't give up. God hasn't. No matter what you're facing today, he's with you, loving you. And he has amazing plans for your future.

*Dear Jenny:*

*I have a friend who seems to be struggling with depression, and she seems to be losing the battle. She hasn't told anyone but me that she's thinking about suicide, but she made me promise not to tell anyone. I want to keep my promise to her, but I don't know how to handle this by myself. What should I do?*

*Worried and Scared*

Dear Worried:

Your friend may not realize it, but she is asking for your help. And though that means you'll need to break your promise, it's the only way your friend can get the help she needs to get her through this bleak time in her life. First pray about the situation, and pray for your friend. Then find a reliable adult to help you figure out what to do for your friend. Your friend may need counseling, or she may need more intense treatment. That's for the adults to figure out, not you.

Your friend may be angry at you at first for breaking your promise—but it's worth the risk. After all, there's time to reconcile if she's alive—but the alternative is heartbreaking.

## DIGGING DEEPER WITH GOD

**Step 1:** Go for a walk alone with God. As you walk, tell God about your dreams for the future. He already knows them, but he likes it when we come to him with our heart's desires. Some ideas to get you thinking:
• Do you want to go to college? What kind of job do you want? Do you want to get

married? Have children? In what ways would you like to serve God and minister to others?

**Step 2:** Tell God you'd like him to speak to you about your life and his plans for you.

**Step 3:** Be silent for at least 10 minutes—more is better if you have the time. Notice the sounds around you, and let them remind you of God's life-giving presence. Some stuff to notice:

• Are birds singing? Is there a gentle breeze? Are cars going by? Are people talking or laughing?

**Step 4:** Be at peace in God's presence knowing that he's there with you and that he loves you.

• Take a few deep breaths to help you relax. Then just be open to whatever God might want to say to you. Often God will speak quietly inside your heart. Other times he may direct your attention to something in your surroundings.

**Step 5:** When a thought, feeling, or object around you catches your attention, just stop and ask God:

• What are you trying to say to me? Then just listen. After a while, you can begin to have a conversation with God about what he is saying to you.

*BUMPER STICKER THEOLOGY*

**WITH JESUS, YOUR FUTURE'S ALWAYS BRIGHT.**

**Step 6:** Wrap up your prayer-walk with God:

   • Say thank you to God. Share your prayer
     experience with another Christian you trust
     and respect.

   Note: Don't feel discouraged if you don't "hear"
anything. Sometimes God would rather we just relax in
his presence and experience his love. Know that God
was and continues to be with you. Don't be surprised if
you hear him speak later on in the day or even in the
coming week. Even if you hear nothing, the important
thing is that you took time to allow God to speak to
you. You can repeat this prayer-walk whenever you feel
the need to reconnect with God or whenever you are
contemplating a major life decision.

## PRAYING FOR PURPOSE

> 66 **No one whose hope is in you
> will ever be put to shame.** 99
> **PSALM 25:3 NIV**

**Dear God,**
You actually have good plans for me! I guess
I should have known all along. But sometimes it's hard to believe—especially when
I'm going through a rough time. Forgive me
for doubting your goodness. Forgive me for the
times I've believed the lies of Satan. Help me hear
your voice of love instead. Guide me in your ways so I
can discover all the good plans you have for me.
Thank you, God.
**Amen**

# How Can I Discover God's Plans for My Life?

God has great plans for your life! That's something to be excited about. But last time you checked, God wasn't posting any road signs or writing messages in the sky to tell you which way to go. You'd love to know what God has in store for you, I'm sure, but you don't even know where to start. Well, I've got some good news.

Did you know that about 90 percent of God's plans for you can be found in the Bible? No guesswork involved! God knew we'd want to know his will for our lives, so he made 90 percent of it crystal clear. And that applies to all of us. Here are some examples:

- Love God and love others, too (Matthew 22:37–40).
- Be a witness for Jesus to those around you (Matthew 5:14–16).
- Don't let anger, hate, or violence into your life (Matthew 5:21–26).
- Keep yourself sexually pure (Matthew 5:27–32).
- Love everyone—even people who don't like you (Matthew 5:43–48).
- Don't be materialistic (Matthew 6:19–24).
- Pray to God to ask him for the things you need (Matthew 7:7–12).

## HOW ARE YOU DOING?

HOW ARE YOU DOING ON THE PLANS GOD'S GIVEN US IN THE BIBLE? IF YOU'RE NOT DOING SO HOT, THERE'S NO NEED TO ASK GOD TO REVEAL MORE OF HIS PLANS FOR YOU . . . *YET.* YOU WON'T BE ABLE TO HEAR THEM UNLESS YOU'RE SINCERELY TRYING TO LIVE OUT THE 90 PERCENT FIRST. SO, COMMIT YOURSELF TO LIVING THE WAY GOD HAS DESIGNED. WITH GOD'S HELP YOU CAN DO IT! AS YOU GROW IN YOUR RELATIONSHIP WITH GOD, HE'LL BEGIN REVEALING OTHER, MORE SPECIFIC PLANS HE HAS FOR YOU.

This definitely isn't a complete list of *all* the plans God has laid out for us in the Bible, but you get the picture.

It's important to know and live by God's plans for us because they form the foundation for all the less obvious plans God has—the individual future God has just for you. And God will never lead you in a direction that goes against the 90 percent clear stuff he's laid out for us in his Word. For example: God will never lead you to have sex before marriage, no matter how much you love your boyfriend or girlfriend, because his plan is for you to remain sexually pure until you say your wedding vows. God knows your life will end up better because of it.

But let's say you have options in front of you that don't go against God's will in Scripture. For example: Who should you go to prom with? Should you go on your youth group's mission trip? Should you go to college... if so, which one? Should you get married? If so, who will it be and how will you know? How do you know what the best option is? How do you know which direction God would have you go? The questions can be both exciting and overwhelming. God does have the answers for us, but we've got to make sure we're doing all we can to listen for his voice.

Here are some practical things you can do that will help you listen for God's direction in your life:

#1: Pray and ask God to help you make the right decisions in life. This is the first and most important step. Involve God from the very beginning. You'll be glad you did.

#2: Listen for his voice. God may lead you to a specific Bible passage that sheds light on your situation. He also might speak to you through your circumstances or through the advice of a Christian friend. The important thing is to be open and ready to hear what God has to say. (Remember that God will never say anything to you that goes against what he's already given you in Scripture.)

#3: Seek advice from older Christians you know and trust. You can go to your peers for advice, and God can most certainly use them, but older Christians have had more practice listening for God's voice. They can help you hear what God is trying to say to you.

#4: Once you get a clear idea of how God is leading you, act on it. Take whatever steps of faith are necessary to see God's plan for you unfold.

This last step can be scary. What if you didn't hear God right? What if you fail at your attempt to do what God is leading you to do? Well, you don't have to worry or be afraid. Just do the best you can. God knows you want to please him. If you make a mistake, he'll be there to pick you up and help you move on. God can use even your mistakes to bring about something good in your life.

> ## GET READY!
>
> SOMETIMES GOD WILL HOLD BACK ON REVEALING HIS PLANS FOR US. USUALLY IT'S BECAUSE HE KNOWS WE AREN'T READY TO ACCEPT AND ACT ON WHAT HE HAS TO SAY. BUT HE'S PATIENTLY WAITING FOR US TO BE READY. SO, ASK GOD TO GET YOU READY. ASK HIM TO PREPARE YOU. HE'LL OFTEN DO THIS BY GIVING YOU EASIER THINGS TO DO— SMALLER TASKS. MAKE SURE YOU DO THEM. THOSE LITTLE THINGS THAT SEEM INSIGNIFICANT OR EVEN UNEXCITING ARE GOD'S WAY OF PREPARING YOUR HEART FOR GREATER THINGS TO COME.

## PRAYING FOR PURPOSE

> **We know that all things work together for good for those who love God, who are called according to his purpose.**
> **ROMANS 8:28**

**Dear God,**
I'm so glad that you have good plans for my life. But sometimes it's hard for me to find out what those plans are. Help me listen for your voice every day. And as I hear you speaking to me, help me know what to do next to fulfill your plans. Please give me the faith and the courage to do the things you lead me to do. And when I make a mistake, remind me that you are there to help me and forgive me. I'm glad that I can't totally screw up your plans for me. You're such an awesome God! And I love you. Please give me the strength to live for you. In Jesus' name,
**Amen**

# Hey, Let's Go for a Ride

" 'Look, the home of God is now among his people! He will live with them, and they will be his people. God himself will be with them. He will remove all their sorrows, and there will be no more death or sorrow or crying or pain. For the old world and its evils are gone forever.' And the one sitting on the throne said, 'Look, I am making all things new!' "
REVELATION 21:3-5 NLT

Let's talk about swimming for a minute. More accurately, let's talk about floating, or more specifically, floating on a raft. Now, we've got a couple options. Option A is a lovely float in a pool. The pool's in your backyard and is very nice. It has a nice little privacy fence surrounding it so you can have it all to yourself. You can invite a friend or two over if you like, but it's your

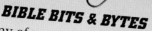
pool. The water is always crystal clear because you've got plenty of chlorine and a very efficient filter. The water temperature is perfect because you have a heater. As you float along, you can get a wonderful tan, take a little nap, pop inside for a drink any time you get thirsty. It's a great pool, and floating on this raft is a really wonderful thing.

Option B is quite a different experience. You put the same raft in the nearest river, and off you go. You don't have the water all to yourself this time. In fact, as you go along you see more and more people, some out in boats, others on rafts, all headed down the river. If you get hungry or thirsty and don't have what you need, you better flag down some passing boat and find a helping hand. Every day the scenery changes. Every day is something new. New rivers join the one you're on, and the flow swells and gets faster. You aren't always sure where you are headed, but you know where you'll ultimately end up. You are headed toward the ocean, and there's no stopping that. This may not be the most relaxing ride, the

**BUMPER STICKER THEOLOGY**

**GOD: CHANGING THE WORLD, ONE HEART AT A TIME.**

242

**Lord in heaven,**

Today, I'm not talking about me or asking for anything for myself. Today, I'm trying to see the bigger picture. Today, I'm imagining myself out in space, looking down with a satellite view of the world. Today, I want you to know that I understand that the world is bigger than me and my relationship with you.

I've been trying so hard to walk the path that you are laying out for me that I sometimes lose sight of the fact that there are other people walking along-side me—and that there are places beyond the path that I walk.

Today, Lord, I ask only that you use me to do your good work in this world. Give me the wisdom to see what it is you need me to do and the courage to go out and get it done. I will try with all my heart and soul to listen to your guidance and live a life that makes a difference. Thank you, Lord. I pray in your name,

**Amen**

current may be too fast for you to take a nap, but you can be sure it'll never be boring.

When most of us think about our Christian life, it can be easy to think of it looking a lot like Option A. Our faith is about us and God, right? God's there to get us through our day, to help us have a calmer attitude about that test next period, and to give us a little more self-discipline. In return, God asks us to talk to him. Read his Bible a little every day, try to stay awake while we pray, and go to church regularly. But in return, we get this nice, safe, clean, swimming pool kind of faith.

The Christian writer C. S. Lewis in his children's classic *The Lion, the Witch, and the Wardrobe* wrote dialogue that captures what life with God is really like. Some schoolchildren have found their way to this world called Narnia, where a monstrously large lion named Aslan represents Jesus. Before the kids meet Aslan for the first time they are understandably scared about meeting a huge lion. One of them asks if he is tame. "Tame? No he's not tame at all, but he's good," is the answer they are given. Sure enough, they meet Aslan and find him to be wonderfully good but anything but tame, and they get pulled into adventures wilder than anything they ever imagined.

That's Option B. Option B is a faith that says, "Hey, do you want to come out and play?" God does not just invite us into a nice little swimming pool kind of faith. He invites us to throw our raft into his river and see where the current takes us. It takes us to other people. It takes us by changing places and situations. It takes us to a world way bigger than our backyard.

If you were the only person on earth, Jesus would still come to earth and die on the cross for you. God's love for you is personal and intimate. God does care about all the details of your life. At the same time, he's got big things going on. God's about

Hey Steve,

I've heard people say that Christians are never home until we get to heaven. I've also heard that the most important thing we can do is to give our lives to God and to accept his forgiveness. Why should we stick around here then? Why wouldn't we be better off to leave this world, which, to be honest, seems pretty messed up, and just go on to heaven as soon as we become Christians? Why does God leave us here?

Homesick for Heaven

Dear Homesick,

Christians have wondered about that ever since the first followers of Jesus didn't follow Jesus to heaven at the ascension. The apostle Paul taught that it is better for us to stay because God has big plans for the world, and he looks to his followers to make those plans happen. While he cares for each individual's salvation, his concern is for the entire world. So, roll up your sleeves and get involved in the exciting work that God is doing all around you.

changing the whole world, not just your attitudes about drinking and picking on your little brother. When we sign on with him, it's signing on for a great adventure, a thrilling ride, an involvement with what he's doing in the entire world, not just in our little corner of it.

This book is all about living a life full of purpose. I'd argue that you could sum up our purpose in life as Christians in a simple phrase, "to know him and to make him known." What does that mean? "To know him" means to enjoy his love for us, to do all of those personal swimming pool kinds of things. Dive into the Bible, submerge yourself in pray, go to church, get involved in your youth group. "To make him known" means looking at the world around you and asking, "Who around me needs to be touched by God's love, and how can I be part of letting them know they are loved by God?" Maybe it's building a house over spring break for a poor family, maybe it's helping with a food drive, maybe it's telling that kid who sits next to you in math class, whose parents are splitting up, that you have been praying for her. It's throwing your raft in the great big river of God's care for the entire world and seeing where it takes you.

## GO OUTSIDE THE BOX

If you help serve at the Salvation Army food kitchen every Saturday afternoon, that's great! What a wonderful thing to do—keep it up! But sometimes you need to think outside the box, or rather *act* outside the box. The point is to do something completely different.

This might take a bit of research. Check with your pastor, look online, ask your neighbors. See what needs to be done. It could be anything that's part of God's plan for you. Pray about it. You'll know when the right opportunity presents itself.

Maybe you'll find a new activity that you just love doing and want to participate in regularly!

## LOOK AT THE WORLD

Reinhold Niebuhr said Christians should start the day with a newspaper in one hand and the Bible in the other so we can know both the needs of the world and what God has to say about them.

Take a moment to look at your school, your community, our country, and the world. What is something (however small) that God would have you do to make an impact this week?

## HAVE YOUR PEOPLE CALL MY PEOPLE!

What plans does the Lord have for you? Big plans, that is. Plans beyond acing your next test or getting your dream date to go to prom.

Try this: Imagine you're having a big business luncheon with God. There you are in heaven at a fancy restaurant, and God is telling you what he expects you to do with your life. Listen closely. Be open-minded to any and all possibilities. Record three things God expects you to accomplish:

1.
2.
3.

### YOU GET WHAT YOU PRAY FOR!

## PRAYING FOR PURPOSE

> " Arise, shine; for your light has come,
> and the glory of the Lord
> has risen upon you....
> the Lord will arise upon you, and his
> glory will appear over you.
> Nations shall come to your light, and
> kings to the brightness of your dawn. "
>
> ISAIAH 60:1-3

**Dear God,**

I thank you so much for what
you've done for me. For the life
and joy you have brought to my
heart. For your presence in my life.
Help me see the bigger picture.
Show me what your cares, dreams,
and plans are for the world around
me are. Show me how I can get in
step with what you are already
doing all around me. Thank you for
letting me be a part of your work in the world.
**Amen**

# A Whole New Family!

" Now all of you together are Christ's body, and each one of you is a separate and necessary part of it. "

1 CORINTHIANS 12:27 NLT

What does it mean to be part of the body of Christ? Well, sit back and check this out because it's pretty cool! And even if you're already very familiar with this concept, it's always worthwhile to think about it and study it further. You may find new ways of thinking about it or come closer to understanding what it means to you personally.

You already know that you are never alone, that God is with you 24/7. But did you know that you are actually joined with all believers, everywhere? You are. God works through family and friends and the members of our church to provide us with comfort and support. In this way, every other believer we share with is like a new family member. We know that they are working as one with God to be there for us. And, in turn, God works through each of us when

READ IT. NOW
DISCUSS IT!

READ 1 CORINTHIANS
12:12–26. WHAT DOES
THE PASSAGE MEAN TO
YOU? GET TOGETHER WITH
A GROUP OF FRIENDS AND
DISCUSS THIS QUOTE.

another believer needs our attention and good will.

The Bible tells us that we are all joined together and that any action of one of us affects all of us. We do not act independently, separate from consequences beyond ourselves. But what does that really mean? Well, for one thing, it means that we each have tremendous responsibility to our fellow Christians.

In the Bible there is the image of a plant and the idea that if any part of the plant is damaged, nothing anywhere on the plant can grow. So to keep growing spiritually, we must all take care of each other—nurture each other and help provide each other with whatever we need for our continued growth and development. It can seem like a tall order to be responsible for *everyone,* but that thought can help keep us on the right path when we feel tempted to stray. Knowing that what you do affects much more than just yourself might make all the difference in the world!

This also means that everyone is equally important to the whole. You are as important as the pastor and your mother and the missionary's kid. You are always needed—no matter what! Each one of us has a unique gift to offer this family of Christ. That gift can only come from us.

**BIBLE BITS & BYTES**

I am the vine, you are the branches. Those who abide in me and I in them bear much fruit, because apart from me you can do nothing.

JOHN 15:5

**Lord,**

I pray that you will help me be worthy of this honor of being part of your holy body. I am here and open to whatever work you have for me. I pray to hear what you need me to do and to have the courage to do it. I wish to act in ways that are respectful to everyone else who is also part of our body in Christ. Please give me the strength, courage, and wisdom to fulfill the tasks you have set for me. This I pray in your name.
**Amen**

*Together* we make up the religious body of our Lord and our faith. That brings us all pretty darn close together in so many ways. We need each other, and we are always there for each other. We've got a whole new family!

## WHO'S YOUR HERO?

We're all joined and part of one family, so that makes everyone from the Bible part of your family heritage. If you had to choose, who from the Bible would be your hero?

Why did you choose this person?

How would you hope to be more like this person in your own life?

## I FOUND CHRIST AND A WHOLE NEW FAMILY! HOW COOL IS THAT?

# PRAYING FOR PURPOSE

> " What this means is that those who become Christians become new persons. They are not the same anymore, for the old life is gone. A new life has begun! All this newness of life is from God, who brought us back to himself through what Christ did. And God has given us the task of reconciling people to him. "
> **2 CORINTHIANS 5:17-18 NLT**

**Dear Father in heaven,**
I know we are one body, but I don't always do the best for everyone. Sometimes I still put myself first, and I act selfishly. I'm striving to live a life with you at the center of everything I say and do, especially now that I know that I am part of you—that we are all part of one holy body. I will try to live up to your expectations. I pray that you will keep me in your sight so I find it easier to live in your light.
**Amen**

# God Can Forgive Any Sin

> " If we confess our sins, he who is faithful and just will forgive us our sins and cleanse us from all unrighteousness. "
>
> 1 JOHN 1:9

Jenny had promised and promised herself that she was going to eat a healthy diet. She had some problems with her knees and was about 30 pounds overweight. Her doctor had told her that she really needed to lose the weight to lighten the stress on her joints. If she did, her knees would stop hurting and could heal. If she didn't, she would probably need surgery by the time she was out of college. Jenny was all set to make a full-fledged attempt to follow the doctor's orders. He had laid out a nutritious diet for her that would allow her to eat enough so that she would not have to feel hungry. She was all set to start on Monday morning. Monday came and went, and Jenny did great! She was very proud

---

**WHAT'S ON YOUR MIND?**

IS THERE SOMETHING YOU DID THAT YOU NEED FORGIVENESS FOR? IT DOESN'T ALWAYS SEEM SO EASY, BUT ALL YOU HAVE TO DO IS ASK. YOU'RE SURE TO FEEL BETTER ONCE YOU ASK GOD TO FORGIVE YOU!

of herself. Then came Tuesday, and that went okay, too. But on Wednesday, some friends invited her out for ice cream after school. She said that she couldn't go because she was on a diet, but they encouraged her to come along anyway—just to talk while they ate. She started out okay, ordering just an iced tea. But then her friends were digging into their big ice-cream sundaes, and she just couldn't take it anymore. Alice, her best friend, suggested that she order just a small dish of plain ice cream. But Jenny figured if she was going to do it, she might as well live it up. Tomorrow she'd make up for it. So she ordered a banana split with extra nuts and whipped cream.

Jenny ate the banana split, but she didn't really enjoying it because she felt guilty. She knew she was doing something that wasn't right for her. Then, instead of moving forward and getting right back on her diet, she felt so bad about what she'd done that she just gave it up! That was it for her healthy eating.

Now what do Jenny's knees and eating problems have to do with sinning? Well, that's great you asked! Actually, there are a couple of analogies going on here. Did you catch them both? First off, when we

**Father in heaven,**
I feel so heavy with the knowledge that I have sinned. Please forgive me and wash away the burden so that I can once again focus on doing your good work. I want to stop focusing on how I messed up. I pray that you will help me let go of the bad feelings and move into your light. This I pray with all my heart, in your name.
**Amen**

sin and don't ask forgiveness, it's like we're walking around all day carrying this heavy burden that we can't escape. It stays with us, weighing us down and wearing us out. We know it's there, and we think about it. This takes loads of mental energy—energy that we could otherwise be channeling toward a productive purpose. Energy that could be used to live according to God's plan for us. Not unlike the way that Jenny's extra weight was hurting her knees and keeping her unhealthy. And the cool thing is that all we have to do to lift the load is to ask for forgiveness. That's it! God loves us and wants to forgive us. He wants us to get started again on the right path.

> **WHEN WE SIN, IT'S LIKE PLACING A LARGE WEIGHT ON OUR SHOULDERS. WE HAVE TO CARRY IT AROUND CONSTANTLY UNTIL WE ASK FOR FORGIVENESS.**

And like Jenny's diet, if we *do* sin—and we will from time to time—the thing to remember is that we can immediately get back to a better life. If we don't attend to what we've done right away, it can be too easy to let everything slide. Never feel that all is lost. No matter what mistakes we make, God will forgive us. Really!

Life can be a rough ride sometimes, with lots of ups and downs. Our job is to stay focused, do the best we can, and ask for forgiveness. Then we can get right back to God when we stray from the path. That's more rewarding than any banana split!

## THE OTHERS

Is there anyone you need to ask for forgiveness and/or apologize to? If so, write their names below. After writing their names, go to them and apologize. Be sure that you are sincere. Be honest and open to their comments; don't get defensive. Do this face-to-face if possible. After you're done, put a check mark after the person's name.

_____

_____

_____

> **FORGIVENESS WASHES OVER YOU LIKE A SHOWER OF FRESH SPRING RAIN, AND YOU ARE BORN ANEW.**

## PRAYING FOR PURPOSE

> 66 **Happy are those whose transgression is forgiven, whose sin is covered. Happy are those to whom the Lord imputes no iniquity, and in whose spirit there is no deceit.** 99
> **PSALM 32:1-2**

**Lord,**

Things are going pretty good right now. I'm keeping you in mind every day. You are at the center of my thoughts and my actions. I am trying to do what you want me to do. Sometimes I worry about messing up. It's like things are so good, I know that eventually I'll do something wrong. There are so many temptations. So I guess I have a three-fold prayer to offer today.

First, thank you for all the good in my life. Thank you for being such a big part of every day. Second, please help me stay on this great path that you are lighting for me. I'm trying hard to go in the right direction. Third, if I do mess up—if I sin—help me find the courage to ask for your forgiveness right away so that I can return to the right way. I believe in you, and I trust in your forgiving spirit.
**Amen**

# Jesus Knows What You Are Feeling

> " O Lord, you have searched me and know me. You know when I sit and when I rise up; you discern my thoughts from far away. You search out my path and my lying down, and are acquainted with all my ways. Even before a word is on my tongue, O Lord, you know it completely. "
> **PSALM 139:1-4**

When you think of someone reading your mind or knowing your thoughts, some pretty wild images come to mind. Maybe you picture some man in a cheap tuxedo at the carnival: Karnack the Magnificent or Monty the Mind Reader. He claims to be able to read your thoughts, but he does his "magic" with rigged trick cards and a helper in the crowd giving him answers. It's a nice show, but if he had to go

Monty the Mind Reader

beyond, "The card you are holding is..." he'd be in big trouble.

A second image that might pop up is from Star Trek movies, where Spock was able to do a mind meld with unsuspecting humans by pressing his fingers against their face and squinting his eyes really hard. After 30 seconds or so, both Spock and

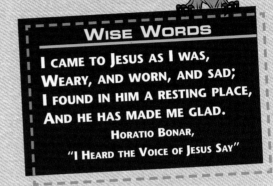

the person he melded with would collapse in exhaustion. But Spock would revive and know what the other person had been thinking. It always seemed to be a pretty unpleasant experience for both parties and not something you'd want to go through often. Plus, you have to be a Vulcan to do it, and there don't seem to be very many of them around the towns most of us live in.

A third and much scarier image is also from science fiction stories. Maybe you've heard about the idea of "big brother"? It's from the novel *1984* by George Orwell. He wrote about a society where the government has become so powerful that it is able to monitor your every move, record your every action, even read your every thought. Some of you may feel like your principal at school is well on his or her way to acquiring this power, but the reality of it would be much scarier than even the strictest principal. We're talking about the ultimate hall monitors, people

*Hey Steve,*

*If God knows everything about me, won't he just use that information against me? He'll know all my secrets and all the things I try to get away with. How can I know that's not all going to come back to haunt me? I'm not sure I want a friendship with Jesus if he has the inside scoop on every thought and feeling in my head.*

*Need Some Privacy*

Dear Need,

There are two things a person can do with inside information. One is what you are describing. It's like the secret police keeping tabs on you and turning you in when they get the goods on you. Any of us would be right to fear that. Another kind would be this scenario: You lose it at basketball practice, and your coach sends you to the locker room early. Later he pulls you aside and angrily asks, "Hey, what was your deal today?!" You then tell him how you were up all night at the hospital because your grandpa's really sick and then you got in trouble at school because none of your homework was done. He responds with, "Man, I'm glad you told me that. Knowing that puts your scene at practice in a whole new perspective. I'd be freaked out, too, if I was going through that."

You see, Jesus knows us in a way that doesn't bring suspicion or judgment but brings understanding and compassion. So don't worry. What God knows about you is used to help you out.

watching every waking and even sleeping moment of our lives. I don't think any of us would say, "Wow, that sounds like a great world. Sign me up."

When Psalm 139 talks about God knowing "when I sit and when I rise up" and knowing our every word, we're talking about something very different from any of those three images. It isn't talking about something fake brought about by a carnival magician. It isn't talking about a hideously painful process that leaves you and God on the verge of collapse. And it definitely is not talking about an intrusive, spying God who wants to gain information about you to use it against you.

You were made by God. He put you together with special, intricate care. He knows you are a guy who secretly listens to that has-been boy band CD in your car though you tell the guys on the team you can't stand them. Or that you're a girl who still has a stash of stuffed animals in your room though you hide them in the back of your closet when your friends come over. The reality is that God knows not only the things we say and do, but he also knows our hopes, dreams, and fears.

Jesus takes this even further. As God's Son, not only

**BUMPER STICKER THEOLOGY**

**JESUS: A FRIEND WHO LOVES THE BEST WHEN HE KNOWS THE WORST.**

does he know everything about us, inside and out, but he is someone who lived a fully human life. He's felt the full range of human emotions himself. We feel fear and anxiety sometimes. Jesus was so frightened and anxious about facing his death on the cross that he spent a sleepless night praying to God for deliverance. We know the pain of failed relationships or losing people we love. Jesus wept at the death of his friend Lazarus. Sometimes, we feel disappointed in or let down by our friends. Jesus experienced the abandonment of all his closest friends at his hour of greatest need.

What does all of that mean for us? If God were all-knowing but cold and cruel, it could be a terrible thing. If God is all-knowing, sympathetic, and compassionate, it is a great thing. If God is all-knowing, has a heart filled with concern and compassion, and has the power to act on our behalf, that is the best news of all! Jesus overcame his fear and bravely went to the cross. He wept over the death of his friend Lazarus and then brought him back to life. He forgave and strengthened his betraying friends, and they turned out to be some of his greatest followers.

Living a life of purpose is no easy thing. There will be moments of loneliness. There will be times of anxiety and fear. There will be times when we will feel misunderstood by others. Add those feelings to all of the normal emotions that all of us experience on a daily basis, and there is a lot for us to deal with. The great news is that we don't need to deal with *any* of it alone. God knows. And he gives us the concern, comfort, and support we need. We can be people of purpose, in part, because we don't have to go it alone.

We have a strong and compassionate friend— one who knows how we feel and walks with us each step of the way.

**Lord,**
I pray that I will not be frightened by your unbelievable power; teach me to let that power inspire me. I will try always to speak to you honestly, knowing that whatever the truth is, you are filled with compassion and understanding. I will open up to you from the deepest place in my soul, understanding that you know me even better than I know myself.

I will work to live so I am proud of what you see in my heart. I pray that you will shine your light on the dark corners of my heart so I am no longer afraid. You are a Lord of forgiveness and caring, and I am thankful to be living for you.
**Amen**

# FRIENDSHIP CHECKLIST

Put a check in the box if you've ever:

☐ Had a friend turn their back on you

☐ Had a friend take a secret you shared and tell others

☐ Had a friend not really understand what you're going through

☐ Had a friend like you more if you act a certain way instead of liking the real you

☐ Had a friend you were afraid to really open up to

Jesus is a friend who knows the worst, sticks with you through thick and thin, and relates to anything you are going through. You will never be able to check any of those boxes if Jesus is the friend you're thinking about!

## PRAYING FOR PURPOSE

> **Depart from evil, and do good; seek peace, and pursue it. The eyes of the Lord are on the righteous, and his ears are open to their cry.**
> **PSALM 34:14–15**

### Dear God,

Sometimes I feel like no one really knows me. People just see the surface when all the real stuff is hidden down below. The Bible says you know everything about me. If that's true, do you still like me? There's some pretty scary stuff in here. If you can see all that I am and still love me, I think I can trust you with my life, trust you with my heart. Help me open up to you more and more each day.

**Amen**

# Dream Big!

> **Whatever you ask for in prayer with faith, you will receive.**
> MATTHEW 21:22

Who are you? Who do you dream of becoming? (And no, you don't get to become a totally different person!) The questions are who do you wish to become, and how do you propose to achieve that goal? Do you know? Have you thought about it?

When you live a life as you're trying to do, with God as the center of everything, you know he will be there with you and for you no matter what. That means that as you pursue your dreams, he will be right at your side helping you along the way. It also means that in planning your future, he'll be there to help you understand and figure it all out. In other words, you're in the very best possible hands. The sky's the limit for you!

Now this doesn't mean that you can just sit back and assume that God will take over. When you've got the Lord in your life, you still don't get into a car on the passenger side and expect him to drive. You get in and drive. He is your navigator, supporter, and safety expert.

Say you decide you want to be a doctor. You've got to work like crazy in high school to get good enough grades to get into a medical school. God can't do that for you. He can help by encouraging you and keeping you focused on your work. He can lend a hand when the going gets rough and you feel you may give up. But  he can't get the good grades for you! It's a team effort. You and God are both on the same team, working together to make your dreams come true.

And when you dream of the future, what do you see? Do you see only the good and positive things that God wishes for you? Or do you tend to see the negative side of things? Do you anticipate difficulties at every turn? It can make a big difference in life if you expect positive things. Having a sunny outlook on life is one of the biggest boosts in achieving everything you have imagined. The more you rely on God and expect life to be good to you, the better it is! Ever notice that there are people who always seem to have things go wrong? They get sick,

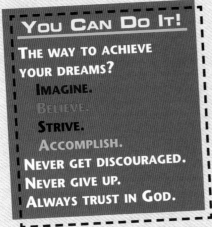

they have accidents, and things just never seem to go their way. Well, sometimes these are the people who expect bad things to happen and who spend all their time and energy complaining.

So, trust in God to help you achieve your dreams and expect everything to work out. Try this: Next time someone asks you, "How are you today?" Answer, "Great, thanks! How about you?" Not only does it make you feel better, but you just might make the other person's outlook a bit more positive. Of course, there are times when you're truly not great, and that's okay, too. This is for those days when you could be doing great if you'd only give yourself a little push.

There are gifts waiting for each and every one of us. God's gifts. All we have to do is expect his goodness and ask.

**BIBLE BITS & BYTES**

And when you turn to the right or when you turn to the left, your ears shall hear a word behind you, saying, "This is the way; walk in it."

ISAIAH 30:21

Say a prayer right now to God. Let him know that you are open and ready for all the good things he has in store for you!

**Father,**
I pray that you will guide me throughout my life. I can feel your presence as I move forward and begin to make choices that will affect my future. I try to stand in your light, and I pray that you will continue to guide me. I pray that you will give me the patience to listen for your guidance and the wisdom to follow the path you have chosen for me. Thank you, Father, for your presence in my life. I have faith that our journey together is going to be great!
**Amen**

## *YOU ARE HERE*

Imagine where you want to be in five years. With God's help, of course, what do you need to do to get there?

1.
2.
3.
4.
5.
6.
7.
8.
9.
10.

# GUIDED IMAGERY

Find a quiet and comfortable place. Take a few deep, quieting breaths. Relax. Imagine a staircase. It can be indoors or outdoors, curving or straight. Put yourself  at the top of the stairs. As you walk down the staircase, think of each step bringing you closer and closer to your goals—to whom you dream of becoming. Walk slowly and feel yourself becoming the person you imagine.

When you get to the bottom of the stairs, imagine you are living the life you dreamed of. Picture it. Picture the details. Feel the satisfaction of knowing that you worked hard to reach your goals.

When you are ready, open your eyes. Know that the place you have imagined really exists. Feel the confidence within you that God will help guide you there!

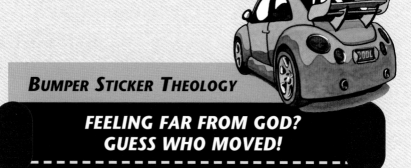

## BUMPER STICKER THEOLOGY

### FEELING FAR FROM GOD?
### GUESS WHO MOVED!

> **WITH GOD'S HELP,
> I CAN BE ANYTHING
> HE WANTS ME TO BE!**

## PRAYING FOR PURPOSE

**Dear Lord,**

Sometimes it seems so hard to even have a clue where I want to go—let alone believe that I could actually get there. I get so discouraged. Sometimes it doesn't even seem worthwhile to dream.

Please help me, Lord, to trust in you and in myself. Help me strengthen my faith in both of us. I want so much out of life. I want to fulfill the destiny you have chosen for me.

Lord, I pray with all my heart that you will help me find more optimism to believe in the future. I pray that you will be there to guide me to the wonderful future that I know is going to be there. Thank you Lord, for listening, for understanding, for guiding.

**Amen**

# God Hears Your Prayers

66 Is there anyone among you who, if your child asks for bread, will give a stone? If you then, who are evil, know how to give good gifts to your children, how much more will your Father in heaven give good things to those who ask him! 99
MATTHEW 7:9, 11

Amazing things happen to our senses when we are in love. Think back to 6th grade or junior high and that first crush. It's as if every one of your senses was on heightened alert. You could be in the most crowded hallway at school and if that special gal or guy stepped into the hall, you instantly saw them. Without even trying you noticed every move they made.

It's the same way with hearing them. You might have been in homeroom and all 30 kids were talking before school started, but if your special person said a word you would have heard it. It's as if there was a special frequency that cut through any amount of noise. After all, they might have said something about you. But even if they didn't, you didn't care. It's just the wonderful sound of their voice, and you could pick it out of any crowd, anywhere, in an instant. At the beginning of the school year you didn't even know who they were, and now theirs was the voice that you listened for and found whenever you were nearby.

Do you think something magical happens to our senses when we are in love? Do our eyes and ears become more tuned for some strange scientific reason? I am no scientist, but I suspect something much simpler is happening. I think that when we have a crush, we pay extra attention to that person, our focus is directed their way, and so we can pick them out of any crowd no matter what else is going on.

There is a lot happening in the world. Billions of people wake up and move through their days. Infinite numbers of things happen every minute just to keep the world from falling apart. Weather patterns move across the world. If we believe that God is

## LOOKING FOR ANSWERS

SOMETIMES WE PRAY AND THEN FORGET TO LOOK FOR THE ANSWER. THIS WEEK, WRITE DOWN YOUR REQUESTS HERE. THEN LOOK BACK OVER THESE IN A FEW WEEKS, AND SEE HOW GOD ANSWERS YOU!

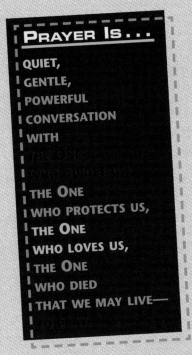

intimately involved in our world and is the one who sustains all creation, he's got a pretty busy job. There's a lot to keep track of.

In the midst of all that is happening, you are worried about your orchestra tryout this afternoon. One friend is stressed about her dating relationship that isn't going too well. Another friend is upset because he doesn't seem to be able to get the handle on those geometry proofs and the test is this afternoon. These are the kinds of things we often pray about. With all of the other stuff going on in the world every second and minute of the day, does God really take the time to listen to our prayers?

The Bible encourages us to present our requests to God. It assures us that like a loving parent, he hears us and answers us. Like you in that crowded homeroom picking out that special voice, God hears us in the midst of all of the noise of the world because ours is a voice that is special and dear to him. That's good news.

Of course, that leads to a second question. If God does really hear and answer our prayers, why don't we always get what we want? In fact, sometimes it can seem like the opposite of what we pray for happens. That zit in the middle of my forehead

**Father,**
Sometimes I have a hard time believing that you are listening. I mean there are so many people in this world, and they all ask for your attention. Some days it seems like I can't possibly ask for your time when you've got so much going on!

Yet, I promise that I will always keep trying—and keep praying. I know that as I grow older, I will come to understand more and more that you are able to listen to all your children. I feel your presence and love in my life, and those feelings grow as I follow your teachings and listen to your voice as I make choices in life.

Father, I pray to you today and know that in the midst of everything that goes on in the world, I am your child. I want you to know that I am here and am trying my hardest to do your work. Thank you, Father, for the gift of prayer.
**Amen**

didn't clear up in time for the 8th-grade dance. Perhaps you didn't make the team you prayed so much about making. More seriously, perhaps, in spite of all your prayers, your parents didn't stay together or your grandfather still died of cancer. If things like that happen, can God really be listening?

I think two images can help us think about this really tough question. The first is from the world of little kids and parents. When I was a kid I loved ice cream. (Okay, I still do.) I would have eaten it every meal of every day, all year long. In fact, that's what I asked for. I asked, begged, pleaded for ice cream because I loved it. My parents were smart and responsible parents who loved me. They knew if I ate nothing but ice cream, my teeth would rot, and I'd be malnourished and obese by the time I left grade school. So, their answer to my requests for ice cream for breakfast was scrambled eggs and orange juice. It wasn't what I asked for, but it was what I actually needed. Something like that is often at work in our prayers. God has a better sense of what we need than we do. We know what we want, but he knows what we need and lovingly gives it to us.

Second image. Think about driving down a winding, wooded country road. In your car, you can only see a couple hundred yards at a time, just up to the next turn. If you were hovering overhead in a helicopter or flying over in a plane, you'd be able to see the whole road. You'd have the big picture. Down on the road, in the woods, driving in your car, your perspective is pretty limited. Seen from up above, you have a much clearer view.

In the same way, we only see the part of our lives immediately in front

## WISE WORDS

I FIND COMFORT IN KNOWING THAT THE SOVEREIGN GOD, WHO IS IN CONTROL OF EVERYTHING, IS THE SAME GOD WHO HAS EXPERIENCED THE PAIN I LIVE WITH EVERY DAY. No MATTER HOW DEEP THE PIT INTO WHICH I DESCEND, I KEEP FINDING GOD THERE.

GERALD SITTSER,
A GRACE DISGUISED

of us. We see how bummed we'll be if we get cut from the team or if that relationship doesn't work out. We can't see the big picture. Maybe you didn't make the team, but you discover that you love and are awesome at music and a whole new future opens up. We can't see that the relationship we so desperately wanted would have been

pretty obsessive and destructive, and we're better off hanging with our group of friends.

Bring God your prayers. You can know that he hears your voice distinctly even in the midst of each crowded day. Also trust that he knows your needs intimately and is looking out for your very best.

## PRAYER CIRCLE

The power of prayer is awesome! It's like discovering a form of energy-efficient fuel that can move mountains. Why not harness that power by forming a prayer group? Get a group together once a month. Have

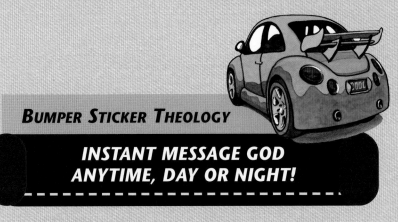

### INSTANT MESSAGE GOD
### ANYTIME, DAY OR NIGHT!

everyone bring prayer requests from anyone who needs prayer. You can come up with general prayer requests also, like for the safety of U.S. military personnel, peace in the Middle East, a cure for cancer, etc.

Form a circle on the floor, and join hands. Go around the circle, and voice your prayer concerns. Allow several minutes of silence for everyone to concentrate on the prayers. You'll feel the powerful energy in the room with you. Totally awesome!

## STRUGGLING WITH PRAYER?

To some of us, prayer just comes naturally. We can talk to God just as we talk to our friends. Others have trouble knowing how to pray. If you're struggling to learn or if you know someone who is, use these steps to get more comfortable having a conversation with God.

1. Find a quiet time and place where you can be alone. (Outside for a walk can be great.)
2. Imagine that God is walking with you. You could picture Jesus, or perhaps you prefer to feel a presence of energy and light. Anything is okay.

3. Just say hello. You don't have to say it out loud; speak silently from your heart.

4. You don't have to ask for anything or say something profound.

5. Let God know that he is in your thoughts and you want to learn to pray.

6. Keep at it. God will be there to help you, and it will get easier.

## *PRAYING FOR PURPOSE*

> **Do not be anxious about anything, but in everything, by prayer and petition, with thanksgiving, present your requests to God.**
> **PHILIPPIANS 4:6 NIV**

**Dear God,**
I thank you for listening to my prayers. I thank you for loving me so much that you are always listening for my voice. I'm also grateful that you know me better than I know myself. Here are some things going on in my life right now: _____

_____.

I trust you to care for these concerns in your great wisdom. Help me recognize the wisdom of your answers and trust in your love.
**Amen**

# Your Unique Gifts

> " Now there are different kinds of spiritual gifts, but it is the same Holy Spirit who is the source of them all. There are different kinds of service in the church, but it is the same Lord we are serving. There are different ways God works in our lives, but it is the same God who does the work through all of us. A spiritual gift is given to each of us as a means of helping the entire church. "
>
> 1 CORINTHIANS 12:4-7 NLT

Do you ever wonder if you have anything valuable to offer the world? Lots of us feel like we don't. In a society that values fame, wealth, beauty, and status, it's easy to feel like a nobody. After all, how many of us are a Donald Trump or a Paris Hilton? Not many! But God doesn't value fame, wealth, beauty, or status. He values *you!*

God created you with a unique set of gifts. You may never grace a movie screen, pose as a model for *Vogue,* play pro football, or run for president, but God has a special place in the world just for you. And no one else can do or be what God has planned for you. Donald Trump owns a lot of stuff, but he'll never own your faith; Paris Hilton attracts a lot of attention, but she's not using it to help people know Jesus the way you are.

The Bible tells us that each one of us, as Christians, has different gifts and abilities that are needed in the world and in the church in order for them to work properly. Let me repeat that: *each one of us.* That means *you.* Maybe you already know what some of your gifts are. Perhaps you will act in movies some day or become the president of the United States. (God wants Christians in places of influence.) So, develop your gifts and rely on God to use you in a way that he will use no one else.

But maybe you're feeling average. Maybe you haven't found anything you think you're really good at. It might feel like everyone around you can do something well except you. But it's not true. If you're having a hard time discovering which gifts God has given you, it's time to ask him.

Sometimes we look only for the obvious gifts; something that gets us noticed—such as sports, music, art, acting, etc. But some of the less-obvious

gifts are the most needed. Maybe you're a great encourager. You can't sing a note in tune, but people come to you for comfort. That's no small gift. What if the whole world was populated by people who could only sing, act, dance, and be doctors and lawyers? The world and the church would be in a big mess!

Lots of people need encouragers to help lift their spirits and point them toward hope in God. And not everyone is a good encourager. Some people are downright bad at it—they couldn't encourage an ice cube out of a frying pan. But that's okay, because the people who don't know how to encourage may know how to organize a group of people to go on a mission trip—perhaps a mission trip you'll go on because you

**BECAUSE NO ONE IN THE WHOLE WORLD IS JUST LIKE YOU, NO ONE IN THE WORLD CAN BRING JOY AND PLEASURE TO GOD'S HEART IN THE SAME WAY YOU CAN!**

feel led by God to use your gift of encouragement for people who need it.

You see how we all need each other? A person in leadership needs support and encouragement from someone behind the scenes. Sure, without leaders the church and society would be aimless. But without people behind the scenes, leaders would fail at their jobs. None of us is more important than any other, and no gift is more important than any other gift.

God created you with a unique set of gifts that no one else in the world has ever had. He placed you where you are in life so you can use those gifts and develop them. So whether you become a senator, an actor, a dad, a mom, a truck driver, a missionary, a teacher—or anything else—God wants to use you to reach others to share the love of Christ. What could give us a greater sense of value and purpose in life than using the gifts God has given us for his glory? Remember *that* the next time you see something about the fabulous lives of Brad Pitt and Jennifer Aniston!

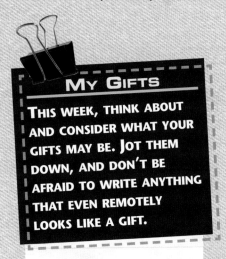

## MY GIFTS

THIS WEEK, THINK ABOUT AND CONSIDER WHAT YOUR GIFTS MAY BE. JOT THEM DOWN, AND DON'T BE AFRAID TO WRITE ANYTHING THAT EVEN REMOTELY LOOKS LIKE A GIFT.

# YOU THINK I'M WHAT?

If you aren't sure what your gifts or talents are, here's a suggestion. Talk to three people who know you well. (Include a parent, teacher, or youth leader in the bunch.) Ask them to do the following:

1. Write a brief description of you as they see you. (Tell them honesty is what you're looking for, not flattery.)

2. Include areas where they see your strengths.

3. What can they see you doing with your life?

Take the input of all three people. Grab your Bible (you never know when God might lead you to Scripture), and find a quiet place to be alone with God.

1. Pray that God will speak to you now and in the days and years ahead.

2. Review what was said about you. How do you feel about it? Is anything a surprise? Talk it over with God.

3. Tell God what your dreams are—what you'd most like to do. (Write it down if it helps.) Do you see any similarities between your dreams

## GO TEAM!

SINCE WE'RE ALL DIFFERENT AND UNIQUE, WE OFTEN DON'T SEE EYE TO EYE. IN EPHESIANS 4:2–3, PAUL REMINDS THE CHURCH IN EPHESUS TO TREAT EACH OTHER WITH LOVE AND PATIENCE. WE'RE ALL DIFFERENT, BUT GOD WANTS US TO GET ALONG AND SEE THAT WE NEED EACH OTHER, TOO. WHEN ONE IS WEAK, ANOTHER IS STRONG—WE CAN HELP EACH OTHER OUT. OUR DIFFERENT GIFTS AREN'T SUPPOSED TO SEPARATE US. INSTEAD, LET'S WORK AS A TEAM FOR GOD'S GLORY!

and what people said about you? What are they? Take special note of these areas.

4. Pray that God will show you your gifts and how to use them. And ask him to help you recognize opportunities when they come along.

## PRAYING FOR PURPOSE

> **Search me, O God, and know my heart; test me and know my thoughts. See if there is any wicked way in me, and lead me in the way everlasting.**
> **PSALM 139:23-34**

**Dear God,**

Thank you for creating me and making me different from everybody else who ever lived. Thank you for giving my life purpose and that I can trust you to direct me toward that purpose. Help me discover, develop, and faithfully use the gifts you've given me for your glory. I can't wait to see how you'll use me to love and share Jesus with others! There's no limit to what you can do, God. So take my dreams for my life and mold them and shape them until they become the perfect expression of your will in my life. In Jesus' name I pray,

**Amen**

# TOUGH QUESTIONS

> " Simon Peter replied, 'Lord, to whom would we go? You alone have the words that give eternal life.' "
>
> JOHN 6:68 NLT

The hardest times to keep our focus on a life of purpose are when life makes no sense to us. There are things that happen that we just can't explain or find our way through. Why do people we love die? Why don't all our relationships work out?

There is one thing we can be sure of, however: God doesn't shy away from these tough questions. We may not find easy or quick answers when we want them, but God promises to walk with us through our confusion and doubt and see us through.

# What Can I Do?

I sponsor a child in Rwanda, Africa. Her name is Nyiramugisha, and she's 16. I've never met her in person. But I know that she likes playing volleyball, singing, and doing art. I know she's in high school, she goes to Sunday school, her parents are farmers, and her chores are to carry water, gather firewood, and garden. When I sent her extra money for Christmas one year, she bought a goat for her family—and was very pleased about it. We send letters to each other now and then.

Just thinking about Nyiramugisha can bring tears to my eyes. Why? Because I can hardly believe that $28 a month buys her a better life. (I mean, $28 barely buys a pair of shoes here!) There were times when $28 a month was a bit of a stretch for me. Right after college I was close to penniless. But I told myself, "If I can't go without a meal or two for her, I'm a pretty sad example of the love of Christ." I'm glad I stuck it out—I've been Nyrimugisha's sponsor for about nine years now.

It's incredible that I get a chance to pray for and love a sister in Christ whom I've never met. I may never get to meet her this side of heaven, but you can be sure she's one of the first people I'll look for when I get there.

My brother is a missionary to Africa. He tells me stories about the people he meets who have AIDS, who struggle in poverty, and who live in leper colonies. At times the problems there seem overwhelming. But then I'm reminded that the suffering in the world isn't confined to a few small countries in Africa—suffering is everywhere! Flip on the news, and within five minutes you'll be convinced: child abductions, war, terrorism, murder, starving people living in filth and disease. The suffering goes on and on. What can one person do?

Well, one person can do exactly what Jesus did—reach out to people one at a time! Jesus didn't just *tell* people he loved them; he *showed* them

he loved them by his actions. Whenever he came across suffering people, he ministered to them. And he expects his followers to do the same. To touch one life at a time may not seem all that impressive to you at first. But think about one person like Nyiramugisha—suddenly sharing the tangible love of Christ with one person seems monumental!

You don't have to be a missionary, either, to minister to the suffering. There are plenty of ways you can reach out to others in your own backyard.

• First of all, realize that there are people around you who are suffering. Mother Teresa of Calcutta, who devoted her life to ministering to the poor in India, used to say that the worst kind of suffering is the poverty of not being loved. Do you know anyone

> **WHEN IT COMES TO SHARING GOD'S LOVE, TALK IS CHEAP AND ACTIONS SPEAK LOUDER THAN WORDS.**

around you who feels unloved, rejected, and outcast? A very simple thing you can do is reach out to that person with friendship.

• There are many, many Christian organizations out there that can educate you about the suffering in other parts of the world. They can also give you opportunities to minister to those in need through financial contributions and other means. Ask your pastor to steer you to a reliable organization.

• Consider going on a short-term mission trip. Maybe your church goes on one every year. Pray and ask God if he wants you to go. There's nothing like actual hands-on experience to teach you how to reach out to those who are suffering.

• Finally, realize that we'll never eliminate all suffering from the world. Until Christ returns to set things straight, there will always be people who suffer. But you can make a difference for one person. If each Christian on earth helped at least one suffering person, imagine what a difference that would make!

# PRAYER LIST

Pray for:

1. Children who have been orphaned by AIDS.
2. Families who have to dig through garbage dumps to find food.
3. Mothers who abandon their children because they can't afford to keep them.
4. Young girls who are sold into prostitution by their families to earn money.
5. People who have no clean water to drink.
6. Fathers who must leave their families behind to find work.
7. People who live in countries ravaged by war.

## LIST IT!

Sometimes when we're spared suffering, we're moved to thank God for all the blessings he's given us. So take some time right now to make a list of all the things you're thankful for.

# PRAYING FOR PURPOSE

> **I want you to share your food with the hungry and to welcome poor wanderers into your homes. Give clothes to those who need them, and do not hide from relatives who need your help.**
> ISAIAH 58:7 NLT

**Dear God,**

There's so much suffering in the world. It's overwhelming to me. But I know it's not overwhelming to you. You have a plan for ministering to those in need, and I want to be a part of it. Forgive me for being selfish sometimes and going for days, weeks, and sometimes months thinking only about myself. Help me be more giving and open to others who are in pain. Let me love others with my actions. Show me how to do it. Sometimes I'm scared to step out in faith to minister to people. But I know that with you anything is possible. Lead me to people who especially need your touch in their lives. Open my eyes so that I can see the suffering around me and in my world. Fill me with your love so I can reach out to others and make a difference for Jesus. In his name I pray,

**Amen**

# How Should I React When I See Christians Sin?

" Without wavering, let us hold
tightly to the hope we say we
have, for God can be trusted
to keep his promise.
Think of ways to encourage one
another to outbursts of
love and good deeds. "
HEBREWS 10:23-24 NLT

Sheila's best friend, Liz, had invited her to a party. It seemed innocent enough. The party was at the home of Liz's drama club friend. Sheila had been told that the parents would be home and that it would be a fun, quiet evening. But when they arrived, Sheila had a bad feeling. There didn't seem to be any adults around, and it looked like kids were drinking. "I don't think this is a good place to be," Sheila immediately told Liz. "Let's get out of here." Liz didn't seem disturbed. "Oh, it's okay. I think they're just drinking a little. It doesn't mean that we have to drink. Let's just hang around and watch what they do!"

So there's Sheila, stuck with a bunch of kids doing something that she firmly believes is wrong. What should she do? What would you do? What would Jesus do? It's not realistic to think Sheila can convince the kids having the party to send everyone home, but she can try if she feels like there is even the tiniest possibility. The next thing she can do is to try to get Liz to leave with her. If Liz insists on staying, then Sheila has to leave by herself. It's not okay to just "hang around" as Liz suggested. Hanging around implies that you agree with the activity going on. And in a case like this, it's not just a personal issue. If the kids were to get arrested, the police would not send Sheila home just because she told them that she was only hanging around because her friend wanted to!

So if you're in a situation where people are doing something wrong, it's your responsibility to first do what you can to see if you can help anyone make a better choice. Next, you need to leave as quickly as possible. Always have a way home. If you can't leave with the person you came with, then have another plan. Talk to your parents about calling them for a ride—anywhere, anytime. It's a good idea to have another adult you can call as well in case your parents aren't available. Talk to your clergyperson and see if he or she will be "on call" for you.

REMEMBER...
WE ALL KNOW IN OUR HEARTS WHAT IS RIGHT AND WHAT IS WRONG.
WE DON'T NEED ANYONE TO TELL US WHEN WE DO SOMETHING WRONG.

It can sometimes be hard to accept that you can't change the world— you can't make people do something that is right just because you know it's right. It's okay to try, but know when to walk away. Don't ever put yourself in danger by trying to make someone stop what they are doing. And if anyone is being hurt by a wrongful action, then it's your responsibility to seek help—right away! That means you can call the police, firefighters, an ambulance, a pastor—an adult who is trained to handle the situation.

**BIBLE BITS & BYTES**
Contrary to popular belief, not all animals entered the ark by twos. Some animals, such as clean animals for eating and all birds, went on the ark in parties of 14.

But what if the sin is something more subtle? Something that doesn't directly affect you? Say you find out that a friend cheated on a math test. Well, you can use the same rules. You can't stop her; she's already done it. (But if she told you ahead of time, you could try to talk her out of it.) You can try to get her to confess to the teacher and take her punishment. Talk to her about the burden of guilt being on her shoulders and how she can lift it by asking forgiveness. If that doesn't work, then you've done all you can. You can't change someone else. Let's say that again. You can't change someone else. The only person you can control is you. When we care about people, we want them to do what's right. But sometimes we have to let go and move on with our own lives.

Can you ask forgiveness for someone else? Yes, you can. "Dear God, please forgive her for cheating" is a great start. This will also help if you want to talk with her about it. You can start by saying, "I've been praying for you," which is a great opening when you're discussing such a tough subject.

No one person is better than another. It can be easy to feel self-important if you see someone do something wrong and you know you are in the right. Everyone is doing the best they can, at that moment. It's important that you keep God front and center in your life. Don't elevate yourself because you choose not to sin. Remember: We're all equal in God's eyes.

## THINK ABOUT IT!

Get a group of friends together who share your faith in God. Think about and answer these questions individually:

(Share your true feelings!)

• Am I better than someone who commits a sin?

• Is it okay for me to judge someone who commits a sin?

• How am I different from someone who commits a sin?

• Should I ever intervene if someone else is about to sin?

# PRAYING FOR PURPOSE

**Heavenly Father,**

I want to do your work here on earth. I wish to help people in any way I can, and I pray you will show me the way. If I can keep even one person from sinning, I know I have done your will. God, I'm here, listening for your word. I pray that I can be all you wish me to be—all I dream to be—and that I will always be open to helping anyone who needs support, caring, and a gentle push in the right direction.

Heavenly Father, please help me stay on the path you laid out for me. Please don't let me be led astray by what I see others doing. Instead, let it make me stronger when I figure out I can make a different choice.

**Amen**

# Please Protect Me from Harm

> " Even though I walk through the darkest valley, I fear no evil; for you are with me. "
>
> PSALM 23:4

God protects us a lot—probably much more often than we ever realize. Who knows how many close calls have been averted because God was watching out for us. But still—there are times when harm does find us.

I had a college professor named Larry Helm. He and his wife, Donna, have three children. They used to have four. Nathan, their oldest son, had just gradu-ated from high school and had a promising future. He and his parents were looking forward to his college years and beyond. What would he major in? Where would he go with his life? Would he get married and have children? How would he serve God in later years? The future was open and full of hope.

Then one night, not long after Nathan's parents dropped him off at college, he tried to cross the freeway on foot. A semi hit Nathan, and he was killed instantly.

Larry and Donna believe that God had the power to protect their son that night. (I know they've prayed often for their children, that God would guide, direct, and protect them.) But the fact remains that their son is dead. Why didn't God protect Nathan? It's a question Larry and Donna struggle with.

They know there are no clear answers—not now anyway. They also know that when they see Jesus face-to-face somehow the question itself will melt away. But for now, they live in the pain and sadness of knowing that God allowed harm to come to their son. It's pain they will live with for the rest of their lives. And it's part of living on this imperfect planet.

Jesus told us that in the world we would have trouble (John 16:33). So it's never a question of *if* we'll have trouble—only of *when* we'll have trouble. And Jesus never promised that we would be protected from all harm. Instead he promised that he would be with us when we're right in the middle of it. And he promised that whatever harm comes into our lives it wouldn't have the last word—that he would take everything bad and use it toward something good.

Larry and Donna are going through an incredibly tough time. They have to live knowing that God,

who had the power to protect their son, chose not to—that's a hard truth to swallow. But they haven't lost their faith. They still believe in a God of love who was with their son when the truck hit him. They believe in the God who weeps with them in their pain.

It is not God's plan for harm to come to us, and it grieves God when it does. He created a paradise called Eden where we would always be safe, healthy, and happy. But we blew it. We chose our way over God's. But God wants to bring us back to a place where nothing bad can happen to us again.

Can you ask God to protect you from harm? You bet! God wants us to go to him with everything. But you probably know that some prayers aren't answered the way we want. We won't know why he allows certain things to happen until we get to heaven. One thing we can be sure of is that when we face trouble, we aren't alone. Not ever! The God who loves us and protects us is with us to the very end.

# COMMONSENSE LIST

God wants to protect us from harm—but you may have noticed that he doesn't stop us from making stupid decisions that could lead to harm. Here are some things you can think about—and maybe change—before you panic and pray that God will swoop down and save you. (They might seem obvious now, but they might not when they're happening.)

**1. Don't ever get inside a car with a driver who's been drinking—even one drink. Never! That's an accident just waiting to happen.**

**2. Make sure you actually study for the midterm before you ask God to protect you from a failing grade.**

**3. If you don't have sex outside of marriage, you won't have to ask God to protect you from getting pregnant or getting an STD.**

**4. Don't go to parties where you know there's alcohol and/or drugs. Drunk/wasted people do really dumb things—and you could end up paying for their bad choices.**

**5. When you drive, don't go blazing through the streets at 90—or even 40—miles an hour. Not only could you harm yourself, but you could seriously hurt—or kill—an innocent person.**

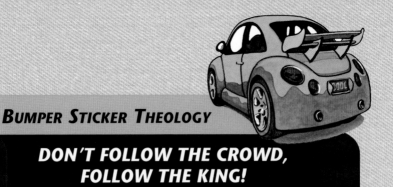

## DON'T FOLLOW THE CROWD, FOLLOW THE KING!

## PRAYING FOR PURPOSE

> Who shall separate us from the love of Christ? Shall trouble or hardship or persecution or famine or nakedness or danger or sword? No, in all these things we are more than conquerors through him who loved us.
>
> **ROMANS 8:35, 37 NIV**

**Dear God,**

My life seems pretty uncertain, but you're always faithful. I'm so glad that no matter what bad things may happen in my life, you'll be there to see me through them. I also know I can make decisions now and every day that will help keep harm away. Help me be wise, God. And for those things I have no control over, I place myself in your hands. Protect me when I need it, and walk with me through the tough times. Thank you that your love is with me in good times and bad. In Jesus' name,

**Amen**

# What Should I Do When I'm Tempted?

Lucy had heard about it before: the whole deal about buying research papers on the Internet. Some kids in her English class did it all the time and never got caught. At first, Lucy thought it was a lousy thing to do. But these days it sounded like a not-so-bad option. After all, she had a major history paper due on Monday, and it was Friday night, and she still hadn't gotten very far on it. On top of her academic stress, there were other things Lucy wanted to do that weekend—the school dance was later that night and the football game was on Saturday. So Lucy took a deep breath and went online and found the perfect paper to hand in on Monday.

When Lucy put her paper on her teacher's desk, she felt a little guilty—but she also hoped she wouldn't get caught. Two weeks went by before Lucy got her paper back. She was nervous the whole time. When Lucy opened the folder and saw the "A" written in red ink at the top of the page, she was relieved. But when she read the teacher's comments below her grade—"Great job, Lucy!"—the guilt came back. "Never mind," she told herself. "I'll never do it again...just this once."

But the next time Lucy was in a tough spot, she remembered how easy it had been to get away with cheating. So she did it again...and again. Each time she got away with it—until she went to college.

Lucy turned in a phony paper to her English professor. Only this time the professor ran everyone's paper through a search engine. Lucy finally got caught. She was called into the Dean's office. Not only did she get a failing grade in her class, but she was placed on academic probation and lost her scholarship. Lucy was humiliated and had a lot of explaining to do to her parents who wondered why the college bill had gone up by thousands of dollars.

Lucy faced a temptation that may be familiar to you—the temptation to cheat on your tests and papers. Maybe you, like Lucy, have given in to similar temptations. But there are lots of other temptations out there, too. See if you can relate to any of these: the temptation to spread gossip, the temptation to experiment with alcohol or pot, the temptation to look at Internet porn, the temptation to have sex with your boyfriend or girlfriend, and on and on. Temptations are everywhere. And if we're not careful, we'll fall into the same trap as Lucy.

We know that God wants us to resist temptations. But let's be honest: It's a really hard thing to do. In fact, there are times when it can seem downright impossible. So here are a few things to remember the next time temptation taps you on the shoulder:

1. *Remember you're not alone.* All of us are tempted to sin. You aren't weird, bad, or hopeless if you're tempted.

2. *Being tempted isn't the same thing as sinning.* Even Jesus was tempted in the desert by Satan. It happens to everybody. It's only when you give in to the temptation that it's sin.

3. *Try to avoid places, situations, and people that cause temptation to come knocking at your door.* If you don't put yourself in a bad situation, then you probably won't be tempted. Know your friends plan on drinking at the party Saturday? Get together with a friend who shares your values. You might be surprised by how many friends will be relieved to have an excuse not to drink.

4. *Find a trusted Christian friend to hold you accountable.* Go to that person whenever you sense that temptation is near. Ask that person to pray for you.

> ## PURPOSEFUL PONDERABLE
>
> JAMES WANTS US TO KNOW THAT GOD ISN'T BEHIND OUR TEMPTATIONS—HE'D NEVER PUT YOU IN A POSITION WHERE YOU MIGHT DO BAD THINGS. NO WAY. THE TRUTH IS THAT *WE ARE* TEMPTED BY OUR OWN SELFISH DESIRES. SO WE SHOULD NEVER SAY WHEN WE'RE TEMPTED THAT GOD IS TESTING US, BECAUSE GOD IS ON OUR SIDE. ISN'T THAT A RELIEF?

*5. Pray for God to show you why you give in to certain temptations.* (This is the most important one.) Ask him to heal that area of your life. Do you often give in to the temptation to gossip about others? Perhaps you feel insecure, so you cope by making others look bad. If that's the case, you need to do more than avoid gossip and ask friends to hold you account-able—you need to let God heal your insecurities.

Finally, remember that God never allows you to be tempted beyond what you can handle. When you're facing temptations, understand that God knows what you're going through—and he is offering his help. You really can overcome it.

## *THINKING IT OVER*

In what areas of your life are you are tempted the most?
**A:**


Think about why you are tempted in those areas. (If you aren't sure, spend some time asking God to show you why you have a weakness in those areas.)

What do you normally do when temptation strikes? Do you give in? Why or why not?
**A:**


Think about what action you can take this week to help you to resist your particular temptation.

## PRAYING FOR PURPOSE

> " Submit yourselves therefore to God. Resist the devil, and he will flee from you. Draw near to God, and he will draw near to you. "
> JAMES 4:7-8

**Dear God,**
You know me better than I know myself. You know why I am tempted to do certain things. So please help me stop giving in to

_____

_____. I really don't want this temptation to have a hold on my life anymore. Forgive me for all the times I've turned my back on you and have gone my own way. Lead me to a person I can trust so I can talk about this, because I know I can't defeat this temptation on my own. And Lord, please show me why I struggle with this temptation. Is there something deep inside me that I need you to heal? If so, please heal me. Thank you for your faithfulness to me. Thank you for your forgiveness and patience. And thank you that you love me even when I fail. I don't even want to think about where I'd be without you, God. I love you!
**Amen**

# If Heaven Is a Party, Is Everyone Invited?

" He has given us eternal life, and this life is in his Son. So who- ever has God's Son has life; whoever does not have his Son does not have life. I write this to you who believe in the Son of God, so that you may know you have eternal life. And we can be confident that he will listen to us whenever we ask him for anything in line with his will. "

**1 John 5:11–14 NLT**

You believe with all your heart that God is loving and kind and yet there's this whole idea of eternal torment in hell. How in the world do those two things fit together? You understand the idea that Jesus died on the cross to bring forgiveness of sins to humanity. Still, you have a neighbor who is one of the very nicest people you've ever met and is Buddhist, and she doesn't believe in Jesus. What's going to happen to her? These are just a few of the questions that we Christians need to wrestle with. These are also questions that don't lend themselves to simple answers. Rather than hide from these questions because they are hard or offer up easy answers that don't look at the whole story, perhaps we can find some basic principles that we can be confident of and that will give us the tools to work through tough questions.

**What we can know: We need help. What we can't know: exactly how that help is given.**

When Christians say that only those that trust in Jesus go to heaven, they aren't trying to be arrogant or say, "We've got a corner on God and tough luck for everyone else." They are basing this belief on some very real ideas. The Bible talks clearly about the truth that all of us are tainted by sin. Sin in this sense is not just killing someone, or stealing, or selling drugs. This idea of sin is that, at our core, all of us think more about ourselves than anything else in the world. We don't put God first. We don't put other people first. We put ourselves first. "You've got to look out for number one." When push comes to shove, even our nice acts have roots in wanting people to be nice back or to like us or to think well of us. Even when we wish we were different, we can't stop being self-centered. This cuts us off from God and causes pain in the world we live in. A planet with billions of people looking out for themselves can lead to a lot of unpleasant things.

Christians believe that since we can't fix ourselves, since we can't stop being self-centered, God has done it for us. That is why Jesus died on the cross. It is God fixing what humanity could

ARROGANCE

**BE PROUD AND COMFORTABLE IN YOUR FAITH. DISCUSS IT PROUDLY WITH OTHERS, BUT NEVER THINK YOU ARE BETTER THAN SOMEONE ELSE BECAUSE OF YOUR FAITH. WE ARE ALL GOD'S CHILDREN.**

**GOD DOESN'T SEND PEOPLE TO HELL, BUT HE ALSO DOESN'T FORCE PEOPLE INTO HEAVEN.**

not. When Christians say that salvation only comes through Jesus, they are saying, "Even our best efforts won't be enough. If God doesn't save us, we're lost."

It can be easy to take this idea, which is fully supported by the Bible, and draw conclusions from it that aren't. Some people say the rescue from sin offered by Jesus is only available to those who speak a set formula of words or experience set ceremonies in just the right church. Those set statements and ceremonies may genuinely help those who experience them to understand what they believe about themselves and Jesus. It would be a mistake, however, to say that we can put the ways of God into a nice little package. On the cross, Jesus extends salvation to a man who doesn't go to church, doesn't say a prayer, and hasn't led a life that was anything to be proud of. We can know we need God's help and that help comes through Jesus, but we can't be sure how or to whom that help is offered.

**What we can know: God desires people to be with him in heaven. What we can't know: who chooses to join him.**

You may have heard people say, or even said yourself, "I can't believe a loving God would send people to hell" or "How can God be loving if he sends people to hell?" I'd suggest that those questions are starting from the wrong place.

Say you get out of college and fall in love. This is the one. You are hopelessly, loopy in love and want to spend the rest of your life with this person. You decide to propose (if you're a woman, it's okay, why should guys always do the asking). You get on one knee, break out the ring, clear your throat, and say, "I want to spend the rest of my life with you. Will you marry me?" Unfortunately, the object of your love has other ideas. "No, I don't really think I want to do that."

What are you going to do? You love this person. You think a life together would be wonderful. And yet, they don't want you. How can that be? You might try to convince them otherwise, but one thing you can't do is say, "I won't accept that. We're going to get married anyway. We are going to spend the rest of our lives together whether you like it or not."

I think that is a better way to approach the idea of being a Christian. The issue isn't God *sending* people away. Rather, it is God not *forcing* people to walk with him. Back to our first question, instead of "I can't believe a loving God would send people to hell," a better statement would be "I can't believe a loving God would force people to be in heaven." The reality is that some people choose to reject God. God doesn't force his love upon us. We can walk away.

**What we can know: All beliefs deserve respect and everyone should be treated with dignity. What we can't know: All beliefs are equally valid or true.**

You may be saying, "Wow, wait a minute! You just contradicted yourself here. Respecting peoples' beliefs means believing that they are all equally true." If you are thinking that, you've got company. That's a very popular idea.

Is it a sound one, though? Say you have a sincere, heartfelt belief in gravity. You believe that if you jump out of a building, you will go down quite quickly. I have a very different belief. With equal sincerity, I believe that gravity is a myth. I believe that if I jump out of a building, I will float peacefully through the air. We ought to talk about our ideas respectfully. You ought to

> **ASK THE QUESTIONS!**
>
> WITH YOUR CHURCH YOUTH GROUP, ORGANIZE A MULTICULTURAL DAY. INVITE KIDS FROM OTHER RELIGIONS TO SPEND THE DAY TOGETHER EXPLORING EACH OTHERS' FAITHS. BE SURE TO INCLUDE EVERYONE. TALK ABOUT THE TOUGH QUESTIONS—ABOUT JESUS, SIN, THE AFTERLIFE, ETC. BE RESPECTFUL OF EACH OTHERS' BELIEFS. BE IN AWE OF THE COMPLEXITY OF GOD'S WORLD!

treat me kindly in our discussion, and I should do the same with you. Still, if I jump out of the building, I will quickly find my sincere, heartfelt belief is unfortunately very wrong.

The various world religions aren't all different ways of saying the same thing. Some believe the physical world is an illusion, others believe the physical world is all that exists. Still others are somewhere between. They can't all be right.

Some religions believe salvation comes through repeated cycles of reincarnation, with the person progressing to ever better qualities of life with each reincarnation. Other religions believe salvation comes through reaching such a state of pure meditation that one's emotional, mental, spiritual self ceases to be. Others believe salvation comes from God's gift. Those are different answers to an important question. They aren't the same answer, and some answers are bound to be closer to the truth than others.

### A Caution

Christians believe that Christianity answers these questions: Why am I here? How do I deal with pain and suffering? How does God deal with pain and suffering? What is our destiny? They believe Christianity answers these questions better than any other alternative. That doesn't mean Christians know what God does with everyone in the world. There are verses that say some of us will reject God and choose eternity apart from him. Other verses say God desires that the whole world be saved. There are verses that talk about Jesus preaching to souls that have already died. There are verses that talk about some people having the truth of God in their hearts even though they've never heard a sermon or read the Bible.

We don't know how all this works. We believe that Jesus came to save us. We can believe in a God who is trying to figure out how to include everyone willing to come to the party rather than trying to make the guest list as exclusive as he can.

## PRAYING FOR PURPOSE

> " For this is the message you have heard from the beginning, that we should love one another. "
> 1 JOHN 3:11

**Dear God,**
I believe that you love me and that you love all of us. I thank you for your Son, Jesus, and his death for us on the cross. Help me trust that you love those who don't know you and that you have plans for them. I thank you that you are bigger and wiser than me and that you have  answers to the things that baffle me. Help me do all I can to spread the wonderful news of your great love to everyone I meet.
**Amen**

# How Should I React to Divorce?

" A man shall leave his father and mother and be joined to his wife, and the two shall become one flesh. So they are no longer two, but one flesh. Therefore, what God has joined together, let no one separate. "

**MARK 10:7-9**

About 50 percent of all marriages end in divorce. Those are the statistics. And the numbers aren't any lower among Christians, believe it or not. That means about 50 percent of you reading these words have divorced parents—and *all* of you probably have friends who are living through their parents' divorces. If you're really honest, you may fear it happening to your family, too.

Divorce is a nightmare—for everyone involved. It breaks hearts, destroys trust, splits families apart, and causes us to question if love can ever be real. It doesn't take a genius to realize that divorce was never part of God's perfect plan for our lives. Its effects are devastating and long lasting. But that doesn't mean there's no hope.

The Bible tells us that God can take even crummy things in life and turn them into steps toward a better future (Romans 8:28). There are ways

that God can help you cope with divorce. And if you have friends who are living through divorce, you can give them the support they need to survive this painful time. The first thing to remember is that divorce isn't your fault. Even if you feel as though you've been the worst son or daughter on the planet, it's never your fault! All self-respecting parents take responsibility for their own relationships. They should never, ever blame their kids for their failed marriages. Your parents probably had difficulties with each other long before you were born. So if a little voice inside your head is saying, *If I had only been better, this never would have happened,* tell it to be quiet. Because that little voice isn't from God, and it doesn't know what it's talking about.

The second thing is to go to God with your heartbreak. Pray every day, all the time. Tell God how you feel, and ask for the strength to live through each

**Dear God,**

Thank you that there is forgiveness for everything. Even for divorce. Right now, I pray for all those I know who have been through divorce. Draw them to you so they can receive your forgiveness and healing. In Jesus' name I pray,
**Amen**

day, every moment of the day. He hasn't left you alone. Jesus said to his disciples, "I am with you always, to the end of the age" (Matthew 28:20). Jesus is by your side and understands your sad-

ness, anger, and pain. Know that he never wanted this to happen to your family and that he will give you what you need to survive this awful time.

Third, find a person you can talk with about your feelings. You need someone who will let you cry and get angry if you need to. That person can be a coun-selor, a peer, a teacher, a youth pastor, a pastor—as long as it's someone you trust and feel comfortable with. Just make sure that person is a committed Chris-tian. You'll want someone who will pray with and for you—someone who will point you to hope in Christ. A non-Christian won't be able to do that for you.

Finally, and this is the toughest one, try to understand that you aren't the only one who's hurt-ing—your folks are going through a lot of pain, too. Perhaps you're thinking, "But they're the ones bring-ing this on themselves!" You know what, you're right. They are. And maybe you're so angry right now you feel like they deserve all the pain they get. But think about how many times you've messed up, with really painful consequences. Let me assure you, this divorce has your parents *very* torn up inside—and mostly because of how it's affecting you.

Even though your parents are failing at their marriage vows, God still wants you to love them. The best way to love your folks through this time is to pray for them. Of course pray that God will work a miracle in their marriage, but understand that your parents have to be open to trusting in God for their marriage first. If they aren't, there's nothing you can do about it. It's not your job to save their marriage. Continue to trust in God no matter what happens with your folks. He is the one person you can always count on even when you get hurt by the people closest to you.

## HELP A FRIEND

Here are five ways you can help a friend deal with their parents' divorce.

1. *Pray for and with your friend.* This is the most valuable thing you can do. You can't heal your friend's heart, but God can.

2. *Take your friend's hurt seriously.* Divorce may happen all the time, but it's still a big deal to your friend whose parents are going through it. Don't let how often divorce happens cause you to treat your friend's feelings casually.

3. *Invite your friend over for dinner.* Share your family with your friend. He or she will probably welcome the chance to get out of their house for a while. Even if your own parents are divorced, a chance for your friend to take a break is a good thing.

4. *Don't speak negatively of marriage or your friend's parents.* Your friend is apt to feel hopeless at times. If you're negative, it will only feed your friend's hopelessness. And that won't help your friend rely on God.

5. *Be available and ready to listen.* Don't try to give advice, especially if you don't know what it's like having divorced parents. What your friend needs most is a listening ear.

## PRAYING FOR PURPOSE

> **Be to me a rock of refuge, a strong fortress, to save me, for you are my rock and my fortress.**
> **PSALM 71:3**

**Dear God,**
This has been a really hard time for all of us. I don't understand why it has to be this way. I just want my mom and dad to stay together. Please help them find strength in you to love each other. But even if they don't, give me the faith to trust you. I put my life in your hands. No matter what happens, I commit myself to loving you and following your will for my life. In Jesus' name I pray,
**Amen**

# Leading a Life of Purpose

> **"** Cry out for insight and under-
> standing. Search for them
> as you would for lost money
> or hidden treasure. **"**
> **PROVERBS 2:3-4 NLT**

**Congratulations!** You've worked for a year on making your life more meaningful—a life filled with God's
purpose. You've read the Bible, you've prayed for
guidance and help, you've thought and thought and
thought about what God wants for you and how you
can live your life in a way that he can be proud of. But
this is no time to stop!

When you struggle with a problem, re-read the
chapter in this book that deals with it. Continue praying for help, continue asking God and the people
around you for guidance, continue walking on the
path God has laid out for you.

You have exciting, fun, and sometimes difficult
times ahead of you. Know that God is with you
through each situation, both the good and the bad.
He's there to guide you and to comfort you. He's
there for you—forever!